Frank Talk

on

LEADERSHIP

Ten Traits of SuperStar Leaders

Frank Talk
on
LEADERSHIP
Ten Traits of SuperStar Leaders

Frank J. Devlyn
Rotary International President, 2000-2001
Chairman, 2005-2006 The Rotary Foundation Trustees

and

David C. Forward
Best-selling author and speaker

Reach*Forward* Publishing
www.Reach*Forward*.com

FRANK TALK on Leadership
Ten Traits of Superstar Leaders

2nd Printing, April 2009

For information address:
Reach*Forward* Publishing
14 West Lake Ave.
Medford, NJ 08055-3429 USA
1-856-988-1738

Printed in the United States of America
Cover design and layout: Ad Graphics, Inc., Tulsa, OK

This book is not an official publication of Rotary International.

FRANK TALK on Leadership may be purchased individually for $13.95 or at substantial discounts for bulk orders of 10 or more copies. Rates are quoted in US funds and do not include shipping and handling.

For more information see the Resource Center at:
www.Reach*Forward*.com
www.FrankTalkBooks.com

ISBN: 978-0-9711030-7-8

What Others Are Saying About *Frank Talk on Leadership*

"*Frank Talk on Leadership* is an important message from Past RI President Frank Devlyn about a subject near and dear to the hearts of all Rotarians. He and David Forward have joined forces once again to create a very readable and entertaining resource for today's leaders and for all those who will become the leaders of tomorrow."

– D.K. Lee, 2008-09 President, Rotary International

"*Frank Talk on Leadership* is a truly excellent manual on how to acquire leadership qualities. It should be required reading, not only for Rotarians, but also for the general public interested in developing skills to help themselves and others to achieve their goals in life of becoming true leaders and better human beings."

– Prof. Dr. Michael Nobel, Chairman, Nobel Charitable Trust;
Visiting Professor, Tokyo Institute of Technology, Japan National University

"Leadership skills are important for every Rotarian, every business person, every professional man and woman. Good leadership is required in every aspect of our lives and it is up to each one of us to provide that leadership in our clubs, in our communities and around the world. Frank Devlyn, with the help of David Forward, has created *Frank Talk on Leadership* as a tool designed to help nurture and develop those skills."

– John Kenny, 2009-10 President, Rotary International

"Frank Devlyn has spent a good portion of his life as a Rotary leader and ambassador. To both he has brought the ambition to serve and to guide others to service. His ideas on leadership are well explained in this book."

– Jeffrey Davidow, US Ambassador to Mexico (1998-2002);
President, Institute of the Americas

"Rotary International has been a model of global citizenship. All citizen movements need leadership, and Frank Devlyn again reflects on leadership's roles and responsibilities—a field he knows so well."

– The Honorable Timothy E. Wirth, President,
United Nations Foundation and Better World Fund

"Frank Devlyn is a leader: when Franks talks, people listen, because his message always inspires you to take the initiative and serve others. Rotary is all about servant leadership—one of the traits described in this book. If you thought Frank was going to tell you what to do each time he met you, you would avoid him; the magic is that he encourages and inspires others to do their best. These are the qualities of effective leaders in both the corporate world and the voluntary sector and I know we all will benefit from the lessons in this book."

– Malcolm S. Morris, Chairman, Stewart Title Company

"As a successful businessman and as a humanitarian, Frank Devlyn has demonstrated outstanding qualities of leadership that inspire and motivate us. His extraordinary communication skills and experience not only make his book *Frank Talk on Leadership* enjoyable to read but also teaches us valuable lessons in leadership."

– Ken D. Tuck, Past President, American Academy of Ophthalmology

"Frank Devlyn in Rotary and in life is described by Theodore Roosevelt in the following statement: 'Far better to dare mighty things, to win glorious triumphs, even though checkered by failure, than to rank with those poor spirits who neither enjoy much, nor suffer much because they live in the great twilight that knows not victory nor defeat.'"

– Kenneth E. Behring, Founder, The Wheelchair Foundation

"Frank Devlyn has written a book about leadership, but it is really an exploration of how we work with each other. He uses real-world examples to bring to life the traits that help motivate others. It is not just about what to do to be a good leader, but why and how it should be done. Frank's extensive experience and interaction with people and organizations around the world, his understanding of human nature and his desire to improve the world around him shine through on these pages. I can highly recommend this as an entertaining and thought provoking read."

– Dunbar Hoskins, MD, Executive Vice President,
The American Academy of Ophthalmology

"This book is a refreshing change from the typical business text and self-help book. Frank Devlyn's storytelling style keeps readers engaged while thought-provoking questions and revelations enable them to increase their success, personal growth and understanding of leadership and management."

– Jim Gibbons, President and CEO, Goodwill Industries International

"Rotary's finest cheerleader, Frank Devlyn, continues to offer insights on the benefits of being a Rotarian. With this newest publication on Leadership, he and David Forward teamed up once again to hit the mark squarely. Experiencing Rotary provides every member exceptional opportunities for growth rarely available in any organization. As chair of the *Institute for Leadership*, one of Rotary's fastest growing leadership training events designed for all Rotarians, we endorse fully this new brilliant and timely book. Take advantage of another opportunity to enrich your life through your Rotary membership."

– Irving J. "Sonny" Brown, Past Rotary International Vice President
and Chair of Rotary's Leadership Development Committee 2007-09

"Past R.I. President Frank Devlyn and David Forward have made a great contribution to Rotary with the publication of *Frank Talk on Leadership*. Emphasizing the importance of leadership development for the future of Rotary and the many opportunities that Rotary offers to its members for quality leadership education is one of the most important issues facing Rotary and voluntary organizations today. No organization offers to the business and professional communities of the world such advantages for enhancing the leadership skills of their own business leaders as does Rotary International. The Rotary Leadership Institute (RLI) is very proud to endorse this great work and recommend it to all Rotarians and other business and professional leaders."

– David Linett, Past Rotary International Director,
International Chair, The Rotary Leadership Institute

DEDICATION

I dedicate this book to my mother and father, who both in their own way helped me find and cultivate those initial qualities of leadership that I acquired in my early years. They ensured I got a great education, and then learned about real leadership with their continual encouragement and help as I worked in the family business.

■ Frank J. Devlyn

I also dedicate the book to my parents, who taught me right from wrong, and the joys of serving the needy, at an early age.

■ David C. Forward

ACKNOWLEDGEMENTS

The authors wish to thank the many friends and family members who have encouraged them to write this, their fourth co-authored book.Special mention must go to Past Rotary International Director David Linett, Past Rotary International Vice President Irving J. "Sonny" Brown, and his Institute for Leadership co-founders John Colman and Mike Adkins.

As usual, Rotarian Jim Weems from Tulsa, Oklahoma has done a wonderful job with the cover design and book production. We thank Jim and Barb for their usual patience, professional advice, and great service.

We are both grateful to the numerous leaders we have encountered in Rotary at club, district, zone, and international levels. Life has indeed been a continuous learning experience, and many of the examples in this book were learned in our interactions with true leaders we have met in Rotary, business, church, and government. We thank them for being mentors to us both.

▪ Frank and David

CONTENTS

ABOUT FRANK DEVLYN

In the world of Rotary, Frank Devlyn is recognized as being one of the most sought-out speakers, constantly in demand for Rotary conferences and events around the world.

His background gives good reason why he is considered by so many to be such a unique, successful leader. Raised on the border between México and the United States, Frank proudly describes himself as bicultural. "As a youngster and student, I spent time in both countries every day," he says. "Home was in Juarez, Chihuahua, México, where my mother's family came from, and I went to school in El Paso, Texas. I was immersed equally in both cultures every day of my youth."

Frank's father, Frank Devlyn, Sr., a World War I veteran of Irish descent, came from a small town near Chicago, Illinois. Frank, Sr., was an optometrist, as is Frank's mother, Nelva. After they married, they moved to Nelva's northern México hometown of Juarez, the country's largest border city, and opened a small optical shop. Frank grew up in the family business, and worked in the store every day after school. At age nine, he made his first pair of eyeglasses.

When Frank turned 22, his father died. By that time, the Devlyns had opened their seventh optical shop. Frank then had to lead the family business with the help of his mother and two younger brothers. In both hard times and good, the Devlyn chain of optical stores has continued to expand. Today Devlyn Optical Group has more than 700 stores and is the largest retail optical company in Latin America, with branches in México, Guatemala, El Salvador, Honduras, and the Dominican Republic. The company also wholesales, distributes, and manufactures a variety of optical and ophthalmic products throughout Latin America.

As testament to his status as a respected, world-recognized leader, Frank sits on the boards of numerous national and international groups. He is frequently asked to serve in a public capacity and it is not uncommon to see Frank being interviewed by the media, Mexican government, or by organizations representing private enterprise and philanthropic groups seeking his advice.

He joined the three-week old Rotary Club of Anáhuac in Mexico City when he was 29. "I doubt, at that time, whether the larger clubs in town would have invited a businessman of my age." He served as the club's third president. Frank describes joining Rotary as "a turning point in my life," and he brought to Rotary the same energy, determination and forward thinking that were hallmarks of his business career.

His blueprint for Rotary in his 2000-01 presidential year was characteristically ambitious. To help Rotarians accomplish his goals and give meaning and life to the theme of *Create Awareness — Take Action*, Frank appointed 20 task forces. Each one focused on work that Rotary clubs worldwide were doing, he says. In a sense, many of these Task Forces were the forerunners of what today are Rotarian Action Groups.

Frank and Gloria Rita, his wife of 42 years, have three daughters and nine grandchildren. Gloria Rita has been Frank's partner in Rotary as in life, joining him at Rotary functions at all levels. For that reason, she was made an honorary Rotarian by Frank's Mexico City – Anahuac Club. Frank is also the author of the best-selling series of Frank Talk books along with co-author David C. Forward.

ABOUT DAVID C. FORWARD

David C. Forward was born and educated in England before moving to the United States in 1972. He is a successful real estate broker in Southern New Jersey and a much-demanded speaker around the world at Rotary district conferences and PETS. He has twice been invited to address a Rotary International Convention. David has frequently been featured in the national and international media, including ABC TV and the BBC.

David is a prolific writer, and has written ten books, including:

- *Heroes After Hours: Extraordinary Acts of Employee Volunteerism*
- *Sales SuperStars*
- *The Essential Guide to the Short-Term Mission Trip*
- *DUH! Lessons in Employee Motivation that Every Business Should Learn*
- *Miracles Among Us: The story of ICAF's mission to Romania's orphaned children*

David co-authored *Frank Talk*, *Frank Talk II*, and *Frank Talk on Our Rotary Foundation* with R.I. President Frank J. Devlyn, and they became the best-selling books in Rotary history, with more than 200,000 books distributed in 10 languages. In 2004, R.I. released *A Century of Service: the Story of Rotary International*, researched and written by David.

A Rotarian since 1978, he served in many club and district leadership positions and is now an honorary member of the Rotary Club of San Francisco. David Forward is a Major Donor to The Rotary Foundation and was awarded the Citation for Meritorious Service for his work as district chairman of the PolioPlus Committee. In addition to his volunteer work in Rotary, David is an elder in his church, and is voluntary president of International Children's Aid Foundation, a ministry that assists orphaned children in Romania. In 2005, the 1.3-million-member National Association of Realtors named David national winner of its Good Neighbor Award for his volunteerism. David is a member of Rotary eClub One.

FOREWORD

By
Cliff Dochterman
President of Rotary International, 1992-93

Libraries are filled with volumes on "leadership." There are leaders who lead military troops, business employees, athletic teams, religious followers, political parties and marching bands. Virtually all followers have a financial obligation or a personal commitment to follow the leader. However, this fourth publication in the "Frank Talk" series, has a new and different approach – leadership in a *volunteer* organization.

Following the style of his previous manuscripts, Frank conducts a conversation with Rotary friends on various styles, skills and characteristics of a volunteer leader. One who leads by personal persuasion, motivation, vision, encouragement, respect and charismatic influence.

Although the primary emphasis is related to leadership experiences in a Rotary Club, the messages and techniques can easily be transposed to a person's daily career and personal relationships. Frequent reference is made to the differences between *management* skills and *leadership* skills. The reader will be impressed with the very practical suggestions for emulating the traits of successful or superstar leaders.

Frank's Top Ten Characteristics of a successful leader provide a valuable check list for the neophyte starting the leadership ladder, or for the executive who has made it to the corporate office. This is a worthwhile text for all individuals who wish to improve their existing skills or who stand on the threshold of a leadership position.

INTRODUCTION

Several years ago, while traveling on a train, Rotary International's then-president Frank Devlyn met three strangers: Sue, Bob, and Duncan. They chatted away and upon learning of his position asked the inevitable question, *What is Rotary?* Ever the promoter, Rotary's roving ambassador invited them to consider becoming Rotarians, but they invoked the objections so often voiced by others about Rotary being a "old boy's club," not having the time to devote to its meetings, and skepticism about one person being able to make a difference. By the end of the journey, they had become friends, and they all joined their local Rotary clubs. Over the next few years, the four Rotarians met two more times, and their friendship deepened as they exchanged questions and advice about energizing their Rotary clubs and becoming more involved with The Rotary Foundation.

Now they meet again as they attend a Rotary International convention. It is an exciting time as each of them embarks on a different leadership journey. Leadership is a skill most of us yearn for; an attribute we hold in high esteem among those who have it. If we are to accomplish almost anything worthwhile in life: from coaching a youth group to motivating a team at work, leading a Rotary club, rising through the ranks in one's career, or initiating a volunteer project—we need to have effective leadership skills.

Rotary provides an excellent forum for leadership development. Consider the young woman who joins a local club. She notices how the "movers and shakers" of the community are a congenial fellowship that transcends all titles, genders, and ages—and they accomplish significant service projects. The young Rotarian soon joins a committee and watches experienced leaders as they share their vision, and plan and execute various activities. She observes how club and district officers communicate, inspire, and direct their all-volunteer groups and gradually she progresses through the ranks into leadership positions herself. The skills our Rotary leader has learned all transfer to her workplace, where she uses those same leadership qualities she has acquired to advance into management. In short, membership in Rotary can develop leaders, and leaders who join Rotary complete the circle by bringing their own skills to their fellow Rotarians.

A number of insightful Rotarians have launched their own leadership training programs in recent years. Past RI Vice President Irving J. "Sonny" Brown brought together four Rotarians—past club presidents and professional leadership training executives—to form the Institute for Leadership. It delivers two-day interactive training workshops offering to all Rotarians an event that helps each participant to recognize their own leadership skills and on "being a leader." The program has been shared with Peace Fellows at The University of North Carolina & Duke University and University of California at Berkeley and at Zone 25-26 Institutes. It is being offered as a community service to other local organizations and in doing so, it improves Rotary's image in the community and opens the opportunity for development for future Rotarians. The program has also been shared in several U.S districts.

One of the most acclaimed courses is the Rotary Leadership Institute, founded by Past RI Director David Linett back in 1992. "I invariably found that weak clubs had poor leadership and strong clubs had excellent leadership," Dave recalls today. "So we began the program to train potential Rotary club leaders. Today, our RLI divisions have provided non-consecutive three-day leadership training workshops for thousands of Rotarians in more than 155 districts around the world. The workshops and courses emphasize both Rotary knowledge and leadership skills for voluntary organizations.

"John Maxwell, who is one of the gurus of leadership, said that if you really want to see if an employee has leadership abilities, you should send him into the community to lead volunteers. That's where we begin our work. There is a worldwide crisis of leadership, and maintaining excellence in Rotary leadership is made more difficult because of the change in every office around the world every year. Rotary needs more than 33,000 new club presidents, 33,000 club officers and boards of directors and more than 530 new district governors—*every year!*"

Linett points to an informal study he continues to make of the best and worst leaders. He frequently asks Rotarians to think of the five last presidents of their club. He asks them to note the best—and the worst leaders, and then asks *"Why were they so?"* The recurring adjectives describing the worst presidents include complaints such as "He only did the minimum," "Lack of vision," "No goals," "disorganized," and "Not very friendly." Those leaders ranked the best were described as being "Creative," "Willing to take risks to launch new projects," "Involved everybody in the club," "Enthusiastic," "Follow through," and "Praise for members."

Each of those traits of best and worst Rotary club leaders also applies to supervisors, managers, and bosses in the public and private sector. It follows that a person who is viewed by both her volunteers and her employees as a trusted, visionary, organized person is one whom they want to follow and whose goals they strive to accomplish. In an era when it seems barely a month passes without a once-respected politician or corporate leader being charged with corruption, the need for effective leaders with a commitment to integrity has never been greater.

Leadership is one of the key benefits of Rotary membership, so teaching and instilling it is an important responsibility for club and district leaders. It draws together people from diverse backgrounds and professions and teaches them how to interact in an environment of personal commitment and responsibility. Thus the young person learns skills in Rotary that can help advance his or her career, while many people who join Rotary later in life bring valuable expertise that benefits Rotary and Rotarians.

But what *is* leadership? Is a leader just a synonym for 'manager,' 'boss,' or 'supervisor'? Warren Bennis, the best-selling author widely considered the pioneer of leadership studies and founding chairman of the Leadership Institute at the University of Southern California says, "Leaders are people who do the right things and managers are the people who do things right. Leaders are interested in direction, vision, goals, objectives, purpose, and effectiveness—the right things. Managers are interested in efficiency, the how-to, the day-to-day, the short run of doing things right." Bennis famously summarized:

"The manager administers; the leader innovates,

The manager maintains; the leader develops,

The manager relies on control; the leader inspires trust."[1]

This is not to suggest that Rotary membership only benefits people interested in management. But the *skills* needed to be effective leaders are, simply put, *life skills* that will help anybody be a better communicator, better team member, better employee, better planner of his business and personal journey through life.

---

[1] *Reinventing Leadership*, Collins Business Essentials, 2005

CHAPTER 1

Together Again

"People have to follow you, or you are not leading."
— Gen. Dwight D. Eisenhower

"Leadership?" Bob raised his eyes skyward. "In my first three years as a Rotarian, you would never have used *leadership* and *Rotary* in the same sentence. Most of the people in my club were lemmings: you know, those little rodents that blindly follow the lemming in front of them right over the cliff. They wanted to go on doing the same thing they'd always done before—which was *nothing*—and heaven help anyone who came in with new ideas. So they only elected club officers who thought the way they did—which was to maintain the status quo."

"That was *your* experience, Bob. But in fairness, I don't think that represents the way *all* Rotary clubs behave."

Bob raised his hands defensively. "I agree with you; that is why I left that club. My new club is completely different. I am finishing my presidential year, and these members are very open minded, progressive and supportive of both my ideas and my team."

"Hi guys!"

We all looked toward the door. It was Sue, wearing a radiant smile, her arms outstretched to give us all hugs. "I'm sorry I'm late," she gushed. "I was actually early, and then as I crossed the lobby I ran into a fellow district governor elect. He is from Nigeria and was wearing his colorful tribal robes. We are cooperating on a World Community Service project, so we had a lot to talk about. Before I knew it, 20 minutes had passed."

It was good to be with Sue, Bob, and Duncan again. Several years ago, we had met by chance on a train journey while I was Rotary International President. They had initially expressed skepticism over my invitation for them to join Rotary, but as I explained the history, the wonderful work Rotarians perform, and the fellowship we enjoy, all three of them ultimately joined Rotary clubs in their home communities. We had met twice since that train ride, and had stayed in contact with one another by email to exchange ideas. Today we were meeting for the fourth time. It was, I thought, a classic example of how people meet as strangers but become friends through Rotary. There was no better example of that than the story Sue had just told us: of how she and a man from Nigeria had met at a Rotary function and were now harnessing the volunteer power of their clubs at opposite ends of the earth for the benefit of humankind.

We were here on the opening day of the Rotary International Convention, an annual event that draws 20,000 or more Rotarians and guests from more than 150 countries and geographic regions.

I turned to Sue as we all sat down. "Well, this must be exciting for you, eh? Here you are at an International Convention, less than a month away from beginning your term as a district governor."

"Oh, Frank. I don't know *how* to feel right now," she admitted. "Of course I am excited and honored. But I am also terrified."

"Terrified! Of what?" I asked.

"Of failing," she said. "I have 54 clubs and 3,200 Rotarians in my district. That is 3,200 different personalities, 3,200 different sets of priorities, 3,200 brains pre-programmed to think, 'Why should I do *that*? We've never done it that way before.'"

"Leadership." It was Duncan who uttered the one-word answer.

"Excuse me?" she queried.

"Leadership," he replied, softly. "Sue, you are about to become the governor of the district, the captain of the ship, the leader of the team. The reason people will respond to your call to action, to do the things you want them to do, to support the activities *you* have prioritized is directly linked to your leadership skills. The same rule applies to any club, district or Rotary International office, and for that matter, to leadership roles outside of Rotary."

The group was silent for several moments as the wisdom of Duncan's pronouncement sunk in. Then he continued. "Look, I spent 43 years with a major chemical company. I began as an apprentice and retired as a senior vice president. Along the way, I worked for a lot of bosses, and ultimately, I suppose you could say, I became one of the bosses. But of one thing I am certain: there is a big difference between being a boss and being a leader. A boss uses authority to order you around; a leader uses inspiration and persuasion. A boss tells you what to do, a leader defines the end result needed and empowers you to take ownership in reaching that goal. A boss uses one-way communication: from him to you; a leader encourages two-way communication—actually, *three-way* communication: upward, downward, and between team members. Subordinates—and I use that word guardedly because, of course, in the voluntary environment, Rotarians are not your subordinates—but subordinates follow a boss's orders because they *have* to. Think of a military officer ordering his enlisted subordinate to do something. The lower-ranked soldier had *better* do what he is told or he is in big trouble. But people follow a leader because they *want* to. Sue, you don't have the power of a military officer or corporate boss. So you need to use your personality, your motivational skills, your ability to sell your ideas and arouse enthusiasm to make those club leaders and grass roots Rotarians *want* to follow you."

"May I add something?" Bob interjected. "I agree with Duncan. He made me think back to a time back in high school when I worked in a donut shop. We had a really awful boss. He came to the store every day and I don't think he even knew our names. He would bark orders and yell at us. We were just kids, so we were terrified of him. As long as he was there, we would do everything he told us. What's that expression . . . *When he said 'jump,' we would ask 'How high?'* But after about six o'clock, he went on to his next store, and as soon as he had left, we would return to doing what we wanted. Thinking back, I am not really proud of the way I acted. But we were teenage kids. We didn't care, because the manager didn't care about us. He had never shared his vision for the business with us; we had no idea why it was important to do the things he was ordering us to do, because he had never taken the time to link his instructions with a value or goal. We had virtually no training, and we watched as he treated all his employees as if they were dirt. So while he was present, we did things his way. But when the cat was away, the mice would play."

"So I hear you both suggesting I avoid modeling the leadership skills of Attila the Hun," said Sue. "I think I could have figured out that one all by myself. My question is not 'What should I *not* do' so much as 'What should I do?' What are the leadership skills we need to succeed in Rotary—or in fact, to be successful in our personal, professional or business endeavors today?"

"That is an interesting question," Bob added. "I have just been promoted at work. Do you think there is a correlation between Rotary membership and leadership skills? And if so, are the leadership skills we learn as Rotarians helpful in our business life?"

The three of them looked at me as if expecting a response.

"You have touched on several questions," I began. "Let me start with how I believe Rotary membership can benefit your career. Say you're a young man—28 years old—who joins the Rotary club. Pretty soon, they ask you to sit on a committee. You notice how some of your town's most influential business and civic leaders are also Rotarians, and despite being the new kid on the block, they seek out your opinion and participation. You notice, and learn from, the committee chairperson and your club president. Gradually, you become more involved in club activities. In a year or two, *you* become assistant chair—and then chairperson—of a committee. You learn from those who trod that path before you, but you also begin to learn about planning, goal setting, organization, recruiting, and accountability. Like Bob's experience in the donut shop, you have already observed the behaviors that turn people off and do not produce the desired results. But you also take note of how some of the members are your community's leaders: the mayor, bank president, and several self-made entrepreneurs; you learn how they achieved their success and you begin to emulate some of their leadership traits. You notice that the people you need to perform for you are on the one hand volunteers, and on the other hand are very busy leaders in their own right. They might be opinionated, more used to giving instructions than taking them.

"Your personality and performance lead to your nomination in the club's leadership hierarchy. First as a club officer, and then as club president you learn how to set goals, communicate with different personality types, develop a team, and motivate people. I've heard some club presidents describe the job to be like herding cats. Yet there is no doubt in my mind that the skills you have now developed in Rotary will not only make you a better, more effective leader in Rotary—they will serve you well in your career."

"And vice versa," Duncan interjected.

"Absolutely!" I affirmed. "I have seen countless men and women bring the leadership skills they learned in their career fields to great advantage in their Rotary clubs. Even in my own company in Mexico, my brothers and I, as executives of a large international corporation have been better leaders in Rotary because of the skill sets we developed at Devlyn Optical. But I also know many of our managers are better leaders of their departments or stores because of what we learned as Rotarians and conveyed to them."

"That's where I need to be right now," said Bob.

"Mexico?" Sue queried.

"No, a more effective manager. I haven't seen you recently, Sue. I guess you've been preparing for your governorship. But about three weeks ago, my boss called me in to tell me they were promoting me to department head."

There was a spontaneous round of congratulations.

"Thanks, but I am scared to death, although I certainly think my leadership experience as club president will help me." Bob admitted. "I never wanted to be a manager. I have always been a techie. Give me a laptop and a high-speed Internet connection and leave me alone: I can solve any problem and deliver any project on time. That's been my mantra since college. Of course, now that I'm married with a new baby, the better salary and benefits that come with a managerial position will be welcome. But now I have to deal with *people*. I don't know if I have the time or the temperament to deal with the nitpicking problems and personalities of the 40 people I'll be supervising."

Sue spoke first. "Bob, you were thrust into the club president's position when Sandy Haverhill got transferred just a month before she was to assume that position, remember?"

"Oh, I certainly do remember it well," said Bob, rolling his eyes.

"The next day, when you and I went out for coffee because you asked me to drop everything and meet you, do you remember what you told me?"

"Not specifically."

"You said almost the same thing you just told us. You said you were terrified at being club president because you had no formal leadership training and didn't know how you were going to get the members to respect you, or how you could be an effective president. Fifty-one weeks later, the club is stronger, larger, more cohesive, more active in service activities—and people have told me you have been one of the best presidents they have ever known."

"I've heard the same comments—and I'm not even in your club," Duncan added.

Sue looked at Bob directly. "Leadership is not a destination. It is a journey. Today, you and I are at the beginning of a journey—yours toward a new career direction and mine as a district governor. I remember attending a seminar where the famous author Tom Peters[2] was speaking. 'Management,' he said, 'is about arranging and telling.

---

[2] Author of *In Search of Excellence* and a renowned authority on leadership

Leadership is about nurturing and embracing.' We can put in place the best-laid plans or, as you told us in your story about your donut shop manager, we can tell people to do things all day long—but that will not make us leaders. And we will typically not accomplish our long-term goals. Yet if I change the focus from me to them, and focus on knowing our people—our employees or our club members—we have a better chance of winning them over. Leaders discover what each person on the team wants and why they want it; what they like and dislike, and then know how to motivate them."

"Frank, you run a big company with hundreds of managers," Bob began. "How do you teach them management skills?"

"Management skills are *easy*," I answered. "*Leadership* skills are more difficult—or at least, more important to learn. Of course, we have a formal management training program. But you can learn management skills—you know, the *how* and the *what* of what needs to be done—from books and seminars. But I believe we learn leadership skills by observing others."

"Sue, I like your analogy of leadership being a journey," Duncan interjected. "I remember Ray Kroc, founder of McDonald's saying, 'You're either green and growing or you'll be ripe and rotting.' I ended up as a senior vice president with DuPro Chemical and yet six weeks before I retired, I signed up for a two-day seminar on cross-cultural communications skills. No matter how long you've been in your position, no matter how lofty your title, you never reach your destination—if being *The Perfect Leader* is really your goal. You can always learn how to be a *better* leader. That's why continuous education is so important."

"There's one thing I'd like to add, though," I said. "We have talked a lot about leadership and titles. Sue, you are looking for better leadership skills to be a more effective district governor. Duncan, you were vice president of a global corporation. Bob, you want to be a better department manager. Yet you don't need a title to be a leader. Titles are conferred by people above you, but a leader is chosen by those below you."

"I've never thought of it that way," said Bob. "So Frank, you held the highest titles in the entire Rotary world: RI President and then chairman of The Rotary Foundation trustees. You have grown your business from a startup to a multinational company—and you still oversee the company. In your opinion, is there a formula for good, effective leadership?"

I again realized three pairs of eyes were focused on me, expecting an answer. "I know it is common nowadays to put everything in neat lists, such as *The 7 Habits* or *The Five Secrets* of something or other," I explained. "I don't know how much imagination it would take for me to fit everything into neat little boxes, but I have a top ten list. As I traveled around the globe, meeting some of the people at the very pinnacle of success in government, commerce, and the voluntary sector, I noticed certain common denominators. These are the qualities that transcend nationality, gender, religion, and the level of affluence. I call them the *Ten Traits of SuperStar Leaders*. Would you like to hear them?"

"Yes!" came the chorus, as if from one voice.

"OK then, here goes." I noticed my three friends had taken out pens to make notes.

> Number One: Integrity.
> Two: Charisma.
> Three: Relationships.
> Four: Competence.

Five: Wisdom.
Six: Goal oriented
Seven: Generosity.
Eight: Enthusiasm.
Nine: Solution oriented.
and Ten: Be a visionary."

"Wow, that's quite a list!" said Sue. "Would you care to share some of your insights on how we can develop those characteristics?"

"Sure," I responded. "We can talk about a couple of them now, and then I have to go to my room and receive a conference call from Mexico. Let's start with number one."

What you need to know

✓ Your own success as a leader is dependent more on those below you in the hierarchical ladder than those above you.

✓ There is a big difference between being a manager/boss and being a leader.

✓ The boss uses authority, the leader uses persuasion and inspiration.

✓ A boss tells you what to do; a leader defines the desired outcome and empowers followers to take ownership in reaching that goal.

✓ A boss uses one-way, top-down communications; a leader encourages three-way communications.

✓ Participating in Rotary leadership teaches many of the skills needed to be more effective in one's business, professional, community, and family life.

✓ Leadership is not a destination, it is a journey.

✓ You don't need a title to be a leader, and having a title doesn't make you a leader.

✓ The Top Ten Traits of SuperStar Leaders are:
  • Integrity
  • Charisma
  • Good at Relationships
  • Competence
  • Wisdom
  • Goal oriented
  • They practice Servant Leadership
  • Enthusiasm
  • Solution-oriented
  • Vision

"Leadership is a potent combination of strategy and character. But if you must be without one, be without strategy."

Gen. Normal Schwartzkopf

CHAPTER 2

A Matter of Character

*"Leadership is about building followership—
and it's your values that build followership. And
it's substance and character, not style, that determine
followership. People follow not just because of
what you do, but because of who you are."*
– **Michael Feiner**, *The Feiner Points of Leadership*

"There is a reason I put this characteristic first," I began. "In my opinion, everything I want to know about a person starts with the question of integrity."

"That's the *most* important quality?" Bob challenged. "That's quite a blanket assertion."

"You bet it is—and I stand by it," I argued. "Think about this: Say I have a vendor who can save me 25% on inventory I need—but I discover the product he is selling me is stolen merchandise. My business reputation would be ruined. Is the additional profit more important than the vendor's honesty? Bob, you have an employee with a personal problem. As her manager, is it better that she confide her circumstances to you so you can get her help, or that she lie to cover up the problem? Sue, I know of a district governor who by all accounts had a successful year, and then at the end of his term took the money budgeted for a district humanitarian project and used it to throw his changeover party. How much respect do you think Rotarians have for him anymore?"

The three of them nodded knowingly.

"You see, honesty is something you can only legislate so far. I doubt many Rotarians would hit an old lady over the head and steal her money. That would be both illegal and dishonest. But real integrity goes to a higher bar than just heeding the letter of the law. I know managers whose secretary comes in to tell them somebody they don't really want to talk with is on the telephone. 'Tell him I'm not in,' he says. That's a complete lie! That manager could have accomplished the same end by asking his secretary to tell the caller he is unable to speak to him right then, but will get back to him later. What kind of message did that man send to his own employee when he demonstrated that it was perfectly acceptable to lie? You might say, 'Well, Frank, that was just a little lie.' But it wasn't! A lie is a lie. When it comes to integrity, the little things are the big things."

"You used both words, *honesty* and *integrity*," Bob pointed out. "Are they synonymous?"

"From my perspective, I don't believe they are," Duncan responded. "You can say to somebody, 'I faked our financial reports and stole millions of dollars from my company' and you would be *honest*—but certainly would not have integrity."

"Good point, Duncan," I said. "I have a friend who started a foundation to help orphans in Romania. When his board set about writing the foundation's by-laws, a national scandal erupted in the USA. The CEO of one of the country's largest charities was found to be using donors' funds to pay for $10,000 Concorde tickets across the Atlantic. That was not illegal, but was it the action of an ethical charity?"

"I think not!" snorted Duncan, disgustedly. "And I remember that incident well. At the time, I was DuPro's United Way chairman and we had just collected $120,000 from our employees for that year's charity campaign."

"So what did your friend's foundation do?" enquired Bob.

"The board realized it could not anticipate every specific act of bad conduct a board member could commit, so they incorporated into their by-laws a catch-all provision: 'No officer, director, employee, or volunteer of ICAF may commit any deed or make any statement that could embarrass the organization if it was reported in the newspaper.'"

"That's a good policy statement," Bob reasoned. "But I wonder if you could apply that standard across the entire Rotary world. I know my company has encountered ethical dilemmas in countries where bribes are expected. So how do you define integrity and honesty in a corrupt society?"

"That's a fair question," I began. "Let's establish a base line. Would you agree, as Rotarians, that the Four-Way Test applies to each of us, no matter where we live or work?"

Bob, Duncan, and Sue nodded their heads in agreement.

"The Four-Way Test, remember, was created by Herb Taylor in 1932 because his company was in bankruptcy in the midst of the Great Depression. If ever there was a time when many people would feel tempted to succumb to ethical corner cutting, it would probably have been then. But the Four-Way Test doesn't say 'Is it the truth—unless you think the other guy is lying?', or, 'Is it fair to all concerned, *except* this one customer who can afford to be ripped off?' The truth is always the truth. Doing the right thing is always defensible. If I condoned bribing customs officials in a certain country, and that became public, my personal and business reputation would be ruined. People all over the world know me as a man of character, yet my argument that

'In that country, *everybody* bribes customs officials' would do little to prevent my reputation from being ruined. Just imagine how you would feel about me if you read of such a thing. Whatever the culture or customs of a country, people with integrity will find a way to do the right thing."

"Frank," said Sue. "You and your brothers have been running Devlyn Optical for forty-plus years, so you already have the benefit of a trustworthy name. You had the advantage of following in the footsteps of your father and mother, who had established a fine reputation for integrity. How do you pass on those character traits to the next generation that join the business? How does a person just starting out do that? For example, there are many club presidents in my district who hardly know me."

"Sue, I think the simple answer is: you prove to people you will do what you promise, and you won't do something bad," I answered. "One of my favorite quotes on that point is from author Mark Twain, who wrote: 'Always do right. It will gratify some people and astonish the rest.'"

"May I add one?" asked Duncan. "I'm the only one here old enough to have fought in World War Two, and one of my most admired leaders was British Field Marshall Bernard Montgomery. Monty said, 'Leadership is the capacity and will to rally men and women to a common purpose and the character which inspires confidence.'"

"I hear two points there," Sue observed. "The first is *rally*; the second is *character.*"

"Very perceptive," Duncan responded. "To be a leader, you have to have the ability to inspire, to motivate, to *rally* one's troops—and I mean 'troops' in the figurative sense. Yet we all know of politicians, corporate chiefs, even religious leaders who know how to give great motivational speeches but who have flawed characters. It brings me no joy to see a famous pastor forced to leave his church because of infidelity, or a congressman caught in a corruption scandal. You are right, Sue. And remember, we can learn how to motivate people by buying a set of tapes, but having character is a much deeper, more ingrained personal quality. You cannot fake integrity."

"Then would you say the most important tenet in leadership is the ability to create and sustain trust?" asked Bob.

"After a moment's silence, it was Duncan who spoke. "I believe it is. I think back to my service in the Marine Corps, and in my years with DuPro Chemical. As a matter of fact, I am also considering the various club and district officers I've known in Rotary. I have seen some of these men and women with great vision—but who never succeeded in achieving their goals because the people who worked with them did not trust them. I'll say it again: you can have vision, make great plans, and be an eloquent speaker, but if your team does not believe you have integrity, you will fail."

"Then what about Enron?" asked Bob, in a rather challenging tone. "I remember reading how Ken Lay and Jeffrey Skilling motivated stockholders—including many employees—to hold onto their shares, even as their fraudulent schemes were about to bring down the company. What kind of leadership was *that*?"

"I think you've proven Duncan's point," Sue interjected. "Ken Lay, Bernie Ebbers of WorldCom, and Tyco's Dennis Kozlowski all had leadership *titles*, and they clearly had vision. They must have also possessed the ability to rally their employees and shareholders. But they lacked integrity. So any success they enjoyed was temporary. Look at them now. Their lives are ruined. They have lost everything, and Skilling is serving 24 years in prison; I believe Ebbers got 25 years. If they had only been able to match their vision with such traits as character, trustworthiness, and integrity, they could have ruled the world!"

"You know," I began, still forming my thoughts even as I spoke, "this is a very interesting discussion. If we think of those brilliant businessmen Sue just mentioned—and I think we can all agree, they must have been brilliant to get themselves and their companies to the heights they attained—when did they go bad? Or let's go back to the TV preacher or congressman Duncan alluded to. Were they always scoundrels? I think of Robert Frost's poem *The Road Not Taken*. It describes two roads diverging in a wood and how he could not take both. One road was well worn, for many travelers had chosen this path. But Frost says, 'I, I took the one less traveled by. And that has made all the difference.'

"Some might say the easy path is to give in to temptation, or to not tell the truth, or to be less than completely honest. But if you choose that path, there is no turning back. It may sometimes seem it is the road most traveled, but look where it led for the people Sue and Duncan just talked about. Clearly, the road less traveled is the one Rotarians must choose; it is the path of integrity, honesty, and trust. And there is no other organization on earth the size of Rotary that can do what we can do with our commitment to ethics espoused in the Four-Way Test."

"I have a question," Bob announced. "Do you think people are born to be leaders or do they learn those skills?"

I looked around the table. "Anybody want to answer this one?"

"The floor is yours, Frank," said Sue.

"Bob, you haven't given me time to conduct an exhaustive study or even think this out," I began. "But my initial response is that leadership skills are generally not inherited. When I think of the people we might consider some of history's greatest leaders: Churchill, Lincoln, Gandhi, Margaret Thatcher, Paul Harris . . . all of them came from different backgrounds and they *learned* their leadership skills."

"Duncan started us on the track of defining leadership partly as being able to rally the team to meet your goals, and having integrity. I agree that we can read books and attend training seminars to learn many leadership skills, but character development, I believe, starts a lot earlier. You have seen statistics that suggest children who grow up in homes where cigarettes, alcohol, drugs, or abusive behavior is prevalent will frequently follow those behaviors upon reaching adulthood. I believe the same influences apply to honesty. We learn so much from our parents—both good and bad. Let me give you an example.

"The wife of a friend of mine tells the story of when her father took her to the movies back in the early 1960s. She had just turned 10 years old and was small for her age. As they approached the ticket office, the little girl read the sign that announced *Children under 10: Half Price.* 'Daddy,' she said. 'They don't know I just had a birthday, so why don't you tell them I am still nine; you will save two dollars.' For that little girl, this was a moment when *two roads diverged in a wood.* Her father gently explained that this would be dishonest; that the cashier might not know—but the man and his daughter would know. Her father was a prominent attorney, the son of a Rotarian, and active in his church. 'How could I live with the knowledge that I had cheated somebody out of two dollars—and had taught my own daughter that this was acceptable behavior?' he asked her.

"You see, if you condone telling a little lie to save two dollars, you are already starting on the slippery slope to ever more deception, to even greater dishonesty. The action you take today will be noticed by others who form their opinion of your character on the words you speak and the deeds you do. Chrissie's father had probably forgotten the entire incident within a month, but it was a lesson she took to heart that influenced her own ethical values as a student, wife, mother, and employee. Almost fifty years after that afternoon at the movies, the lesson in integrity she learned from her father still shapes her character."

"Let me read you something," said Sue, pulling a newspaper clipping from her bag. "The day after I was named governor nominee, a friend in California sent me this article by Kevin Grauman in the *East Bay Business Times*. He wrote, 'Leaders regularly demonstrate a high correlation between their core behaviors, beliefs, and principles and those they expect to be present in their followers. Consequently, leadership embodies the persona of the leader.' I took that to mean that if we as Rotarians truly embrace and adopt such standards as The Four-Way Test in everything we think, say, or do, then integrity is not something I turn on when I go to Rotary. It should be a part of my very persona; of who I am. I know those in my district who chose me as their leader expect it of me, and I expect nothing less of them."

"I agree with you, Sue," I said. "The sad question is, 'Why would some people find your premise remarkable?'"

"Because of the society in which we live today," Duncan reasoned. "We live in an age when honesty is considered unusual. Last week, I was driving my grandson home from school. We stopped at a convenience store so he could buy a cold drink. As we pulled away from the shop, the cashier ran out into the parking lot waving her arms. My grandson had forgotten to pick up his change—48 cents—from the counter. Yesterday, I drove him home again and he asked if we could stop for ice cream. 'I would like to go to that store, granddad," he told me. "Because they have nice, honest people working there.' How sad is it that this simple act was so unusual that it stood out in his mind? Yet it became a great opportunity for me to use the incident as a teaching tool on the drive home."

"All of us know people who are not particularly trustworthy," I began. "How do you like them?"

"Like them?" Bob repeated. "Not much."

"I can think of a couple of people in that category," Sue added. "I don't trust them as far as I can throw them."

"I agree," said Duncan. "Once I've caught you in a lie or dishonest act, I don't even want to be in the same room as you. I have been called an absolutist at times, and this is one of those occasions when integrity, to me, is a black-or-white matter. Either you are honest, or you are not, in my opinion."

"Okay, I hear unanimous agreement," I summarized. "Now, imagine if the person you just thought about became your boss, or your club president, or district governor. What would you do?"

They looked at one another. Bob spoke first. "Well, Frank, I would like to say 'I would quit.' But in fact, I love my job, so I don't think I would resign. I really enjoy Rotary, too, so I cannot see leaving the club, either. If it got really bad, I suppose I would leave, but otherwise I would just hunker down and do my job."

"Would you be as excited about it as you are today?"

"Heck, no! I would show up, do what I needed to do, and leave. I don't want to go the extra distance for somebody I cannot trust."

"That is what happened the year Mike was our club president, remember?" said Sue, looking at Bob. "I was on the board that year and we caught him outright lying. The club lost members and accomplished absolutely nothing that year, because nobody wanted to follow him. I was one of those who proposed we ask him to leave, but the majority on the board believed we had had poor presidents before and that the club could survive another one."

"I am now president of our local Red Cross chapter," said Duncan. "My predecessor was a man who wanted the job for the title, I think. He was verbally abusive to the volunteers and would pit one board member against another to advance his own interests. We suspected he was stealing money, too. Yet because the board was scared of his temper, and their lack of solid evidence of his misappropriations, they let him stay. In two years, we lost 80 volunteers and two of our major fund raising activities had to be canceled for lack of participation. He had the title all right, but nobody wanted anything to do with him."

"You have all made my point," I said, sitting back in my chair. "There are as many different definitions of leadership as there are leadership positions, but *effective* leadership begins with integrity. Without an honest, trustworthy character, everything else is just bullet points on a list. Nobody wants to perform as a team member for a leader they do not trust. But show me a person with the core principles and beliefs embodied in the Rotary value system and I will show you a person ready to learn to lead.

"Now, I noticed you took notes when I gave you my Top Ten Traits of SuperStar Leaders. Who remembers what number two is?"

Sue flipped through her notebook. "Charisma!" she called out triumphantly.

"And Sue is our no-prize winner of the day," I said, laughing.

What you need to know

✓ "Everything I want to know about a person starts with the question of integrity."

✓ Real honesty is more than just heeding the letter of the law.

✓ Never do or say anything that would embarrass you if it appeared in the newspaper.

✓ No matter the country or the culture, people with integrity always do the right thing.

✓ The Four-Way Test still applies to everything we think, say, or do.

✓ Character inspires confidence.

✓ The most important tenet in leadership is the ability to create and sustain trust.

✓ If others are choosing the wrong path, leaders with character take *the road less traveled.*

✓ Leadership skills are *learned*, not inherited.

✓ Leaders demonstrate a high correlation between their own core values and behaviors and those they expect their followers to embody.

✓ It only takes one incident that illustrates lack of trust or integrity to destroy the trust of those who witnessed it.

"I am a man of fixed and unbending principles, the first of which is to be flexible at all times."

Everett Dirksen, US Senator

CHAPTER 3

Charisma

"Charisma is a tricky thing. Jack Kennedy oozed it—but so did Hitler and Charles Manson. Con artists, charlatans, and megalomaniacs can make it their instrument as effectively as the best CEO's entertainers, and Presidents. Used wisely, it's a blessing; indulged, it can be a curse. Charismatic visionaries lead people ahead—and sometimes astray."
– Fortune, **January 15, 1996**

"Charisma. What do you think I mean by that?" I asked.

"A nice personality. A likeable, outgoing person," Bob suggested.

"Exactly. To put it another way, we follow people we like. People will vote for politicians without being able to describe a single one of their policy platforms—because they like the way the candidate comes across on television. Now, don't get me wrong, I am not suggesting that a complete air head would make a good leader . . ."

"Wait, he'd have to be an *ethical* air head, since we are on number two, right?" Sue interjected. We laughed.

"Let's stay with the political scenario for a moment. We have seen people run for high office with unimpeachable integrity and brilliant minds, but they had no charisma. And so they never connected with the voters. Then we had others who resonated with the public because of their magnetic personalities. I am not making any political endorsement here, but think of such presidents as Kennedy, Reagan, and Clinton: they got elected, in large part, because they were able to articulate their vision and people saw them as likeable.

"Now, when we define charisma as a leadership quality in the context of our discussion today, we are talking about the ability to communicate and act in ways that inspire followers. Unlike many other management skills, charisma is an easy attribute to spot but a difficult one to learn. I don't know of a one-day seminar that teaches charisma!

"Yet while I stand by my belief that the most effective leaders are charismatic personalities, charisma alone is not enough. Charisma without ethical values leads to scandal, charisma without vision causes stagnation; charisma without goal setting and planning leads to failure of any meaningful achievement. There is one further risk, one that we have seen with our national leaders and even within Rotary: what happens to the organization after a dynamic, charismatic leader passes the gavel to his or her successor who has a weaker personality? This can cause the followers to feel disillusioned and less inclined to follow the new leader's agenda."

"We just sold our house and bought a new one," said Bob. "We decided to interview four real estate agents and pick the one who would give us the highest price for our home and the lowest commission. The first agent had an impressive resume: she was the top real estate salesperson in our town. But all she talked about was herself and her accomplishments. Agent number two based his entire presentation on how he would discount his commission. When he discovered who had preceded him, he made several uncomplimentary comments about her and showed us we would save three thousand dollars by giving him the listing. Obviously, we would like to save money, but he assumed our bottom line would be all that mattered; he never developed rapport with us, never asked what our motivation for selling was, he never really *connected* with us. But the third agent was wonderful. She exuded charisma. From the moment we met her, she seemed warm, friendly, and sincere. She focused most of her attention on *us*: why we were moving, what we liked most about our neighborhood, what our timeline was, and so on. She showed us she was capable, but more importantly, she showed us she cared. We had to let the fourth agent in because we had already given him the appointment. But the truth is, we couldn't wait for him to leave, because we had decided on the third agent within 15 minutes of meeting her."

"So are you saying the $3,000 saved with the discount broker and the sales track record of the first agent was worth less to you than the comfort level you had with the third broker?" Duncan asked.

"Absolutely!" Bob affirmed. "What's that old adage, *I don't care how much you know until I know how much you care.* Cathy had the magnetism to win us over, and then showed us she was also competent to handle the job."

"We are getting a little off track with this discussion of selling skills, aren't we?" asked Sue.

"I disagree," I replied. "We were talking about how charisma is essential to effective leadership. In a way, leadership skills and selling skills are synonymous. Leadership skills are not just helpful for people with leadership title. Traits such as integrity, charisma, communications skills, vision, and so on help each of us throughout our entire adult lives. Whether we already *have* a leadership title or we aspire to grow into one, these are skills that will help us."

"When I think back to my 43 years with DuPro, I never saw a person who did not perform better under a manager with charisma than under one with a bland or autocratic style," said Duncan. "In fact, I just remembered something. Several years ago, the company sent me to take over a department that had been headed by a brilliant manager, but who could not hold on to employees. We brought in a consultant and he told us, 'People quit people, not companies. We have conducted exit interviews with several of that manager's former employees and every one of them said they loved working for DuPro; they just couldn't stand working with him.' It is the same with Rotary clubs. I remember a few years ago when Bob was ready to quit Rotary, and, if I recall it correctly, it wasn't because he disliked Rotary, it was because he didn't feel any warmth from the club president and the clique that ran the club."

Bob nodded. "You're right, Duncan."

"We cannot at once be autocratic *and* charismatic leaders," I explained. "One of the most influential books for me was Tom Peters' *In Search of Excellence*. In it, he describes the principle he calls MBWA: Managing By Wandering Around. This had a huge impact on me. I realized that for me to truly understand my people, their labor issues, quality control, process improvement ideas and so on, I needed to get out from behind my executive desk and spend more time with them. So from that day until this, I devote part of every day wandering around—unannounced—through every department and visiting many of our retail stores. I want to know my people: I ask about their families, how they like their jobs, what ideas they have for us to be a better company. They know I am there not to check up on them; I am there because I care. I eat in the same cafeteria as they eat, and every one of our 3,500 employees in 600-

plus locations knows they can always come and talk to me or a family member.

"You see, *relationships* are the key to developing people to their fullest potential, so while most supervisors have what we call *position power*, the leader knows how to develop *relationship power*. To accomplish that, we need to understand that the other person likely will have emotions, perceptions, prejudices, outlooks, goals, and attitudes that differ from ours. I remember attending a workshop conducted by the Institute for Leadership and they asked each participant to close their eyes and picture a brown and white dog. Then we had to describe what we saw to the person sitting next to us. Guess what? We has 24 people in the room and there were 24 different descriptions! How difficult was that assignment? A brown and white dog is a brown and white dog! And yet each person brought a different perception with them and so we had large dogs and small dogs and every variety of breed and coloration and hair length imaginable."

Bob was smiling, as if he wanted me to finish so he could say something. "It's funny you cited Tom Peters, Frank, because he is my favorite business author. A couple of years ago, I read his book, *The Brand You*. In it, Peters says that no matter the name or size of the company you work for, to survive and thrive in the new economy, we should consider ourselves to be our own brand: the Brand You. Just as the megabrands succeed or fail based on the public's perception of their brand, so the individuals we work with will like us—or avoid us—directly as a consequence of how they perceive our brand. So our words, our actions, our charisma all contribute to how they see the brand me."

"Do you think The Brand You concept works in Rotary?" asked Sue.

"Yes, I do," said Bob. "In fact, I have already implemented many of the book's suggestions in my year as club president."

"How so?" I enquired.

"I want to be careful how I say this," Bob began. "I decided regardless of whether the district governor or R.I. President were good or bad, *I* was responsible for my club. So I created The Brand You in my mind, committing myself to being the best leader I could possibly be. I am responsible for my brand. That forces me to be pleasant, engaging, and member-oriented. I suppose one could call that charisma."

"So let's summarize this charisma thing," I said. "We define charisma as that part of our personality that communicates warmth, trust, and likeability. Having charisma is generally considered a valuable attribute for leaders, who use their superior communications ability to give easy-to-understand metaphors or anecdotes that distill their ideas into simple messages. The perfect example is Dr. Martin Luther King and his 'I have a dream' speech. I would also call charismatic leaders optimists, confident, solution-oriented, friendly—sometimes even rebels who think outside the box.

"But—and it is an important *but*—having charisma does not guarantee success. Charismatic leaders, who by their nature often tend to be risk-takers, could motivate the team to accomplish the wrong outcomes. And in some organizations, and I am thinking of a scientific setting, the left-brain followers might resent and distrust a charismatic right-brain leader, considering him to be shallow and one-dimensional.'

"*Now,* since we are communicating so well, let's talk next about my Rule Number Three: Being a Great Communicator."

What you need to know

✓ Charisma is part of our personality that communicates warmth, trust, and likeability.

✓ We follow people we like.

✓ Charismatic leaders articulate their vision and resonate with their followers.

✓ Charisma is important—but charisma alone does not make a leader.

✓ It is important to plan for succession after a charismatic leader steps down.

✓ Leaders never forget the adage, "They don't care how much you know until they know how much you care."

✓ "People quit people, not companies."

✓ Leaders practice MBWA: *Managing By Wandering Around.*

✓ Charismatic leaders tend to be risk-takers.

✓ A leader with strong charisma may not be so effective with some personality types and work groups.

*"I suppose leadership
at one time meant muscles,
but today it means getting
along with people."*

Mohandas Gandhi

CHAPTER 4

Communicating
for Success

*"The most important single ingredient
in the formula of success is knowing
how to get along with people."*
– Theodore Roosevelt

"It seems we all have perfect communications skills in hindsight," Sue volunteered.

"What do you mean?" asked Bob.

"Have you ever missed an appointment, or gotten into an argument, because of something someone said—only to discover one or both parties had misunderstood the other?"

"Who hasn't?" said Duncan, as we all nodded in agreement.

"After the problem has occurred, we look back at why it happened and can see how easily we misunderstood one another. I think back to when I was club president. I made my plans, outlined them to the board and then the membership, and began my year like a bullet out of a gun. Two months later, we were no closer to reaching my goals than when the year began. I was frustrated, angry, disappointed—and from the passive resistance I encountered in my club, I think many of my fellow Rotarians felt the same way towards me."

"But Sue," Bob interjected. "You are one of the nicest people I have ever known. If club members were upset with your leadership style, it was *their* fault, not yours."

"Thank you," she said, smiling appreciatively. "But you're wrong. The responsibility is on the leader to ensure she is communicating well. My mistake was to go to PETS, visit other successful clubs, attend a Rotary International Convention, and then try to take my enthusiasm and ideas to the club members all at once. You see, I now realize that to be a good communicator, I have to understand my audience and deliver a message in a format that they will accept. If we have 40 members in a Rotary club, or if you have 40 employees who report to you, we must recognize they have potentially 40 different priorities; they are motivated by 40 different values. I can think of one member of our club whose biggest dream is to double the size of our membership. Another guy left his first Rotary club and is driven to now beat his former club in every respect. Others don't care much about district or international programs; they see Rotary as a social fellowship. Even you, Bob, became almost obsessed with raising money for The Rotary Foundation after you helped with the PolioPlus immunization day in India.

"So there I was, telling them what *I* wanted to do as the new club president, and my ideas were falling on deaf ears. Why? Because I made it about me. I forgot to take the time to discover what *their* vision and passion was. I don't care whether you are talking to your Rotary club member, your employee, or your kid: you dramatically increase your chances of successfully communicating with them if you talk about a topic or value in which they are interested."

"When I speak to our management trainee classes, I draw a graphic on the board," I said, pulling out a pen to illustrate my point on a napkin. "It has three interlocking circles, like this. I write *Your values* inside one circle, then *Customer's values* inside the middle circle, and *Our organization's values* in the third circle. You will notice the three sets of values are interlocked. For me to be an effective leader of Devlyn Optical, I must be intimately familiar with my customer's values—and those of my employees. If my employee understands what we want of him or her, but they ignore the customer's values—we have dislocated the three circles. At best, our corporate communications fail to get across to the customer; at worst, we go out of business. But I can take those same three circles and change the words inside to apply to the Rotary model—or almost any other organization. As Rotary International president, or as district governor, club officer or department head, I need to at once understand the organization's values, the values of the person I am talking to, and those of our 'customer'—in this case, the customer is the grass-roots Rotarian."

"I like the analogy," said Duncan. "I can think of an example that perfectly illustrates your concept: the airline industry. On the one hand, you have carriers like Southwest, JetBlue, and Virgin Atlantic. They treat their employees well, and in turn, the workers make every customer feel good about using that company. On the other hand, you have airlines that spend millions of dollars advertising slogans with claims to be *Something special in the air*, or *The friendly skies*, or that *We begin with You*. But they are *awful*. Why?

Because while management of those companies has padded its nest with lucrative compensation packages, they have cut employee benefits and salaries—and the workers feel they have been lied to and cheated. There is a complete disconnect between the three circles you just described."

"So before I deliver a message, I should first try to understand the audience to whom I am directing it, and second, I should ensure my message is aligned with their values," Bob summarized.

"If you want to increase your chances of communicating *successfully*," said Sue.

"That's another one of Covey's *7 Habits of Highly Effective People*," I reminded them. "'Seek first to understand before seeking to be understood.'"

"I'm sorry to keep bringing up my career at DuPro, but I learned a lot by observing leadership styles during my 43 years there," said Duncan. "The first point I want to make is to emphasize what Sue said about knowing your audience. I think she was talking about 'audience' in the literal sense, but it made me think about some real communications problems I encountered in my early career. I am an engineer by training. I'm not emotive; I'm analytical by nature. Yet I had people who worked with me with completely different personality types. I considered the person in our department who knew everybody's birthday and who came around with cards when anybody was sick to be a timewaster—well, frankly, I thought she was just soft. We had another guy in sales who was always the life of the party, but I considered him shallow and I just didn't have the patience to listen to his jokes. The problem occurred when I became the supervisor, because I had to coach each one of them to better performance. Thanks to some training in the Keirsey and Myers-Briggs personality profile programs, I learned that it is critically important for me to try to understand the personality type of each team member. If he was another analytical, I needed to show him the significance of my message. If it was an amiable type, I would speak softer, smile more, and perhaps enquire about how they were doing. If the person was an autocratic type, as was the case with my boss, I knew he was motivated by results, the bottom line—and was stressed by time wasters. So I would ask for a minute—and take exactly a minute. I would typically communicate with him by getting directly to the point and, knowing that personality type would make the conversation outcome oriented."

"So I hear you saying that you didn't try to copy the other person's style, because that would make you seem fake, but you identified their personality type so you could communicate with them better?" Sue clarified.

"That's right, Sue. But I would like to add another point. I am a real student of history, and I believe we can learn a lot from how some of our country's great leaders have communicated their message. In both the corporate world and the political arena, some leaders chose to communicate through persuasion while others used coercion. Both types had the *authority*, but the leaders who exercised their authority as persuaders were able to develop loyal, enthusiastic teams. Those who chose a dictatorial communications style were far less successful in developing a loyal team or one that met its objectives."

"Can you give us an example of that?" I asked.

Duncan reflected for a moment and then replied: "Sure. Look at a couple of American presidents. Nixon was coercive, dictatorial, and secretive. People followed him when they had to—because he had the executive authority. Compare him to Abraham Lincoln—a leader during the most tumultuous, divisive time in American history. Lincoln also had the executive authority, yet he made almost every important decision by being persuasive, inclusive—always trying to understand all points of view."

"Now *I* get to quote Steven Covey," said Bob. "My boss has been mentoring me recently, and he gave me some great advice that he learned from a Covey seminar he attended. He said we should imagine each person who deals with us has an emotional bank account, and every time we communicate with them, we are either making a deposit or a withdrawal from their bank account. So let's say I catch a team member making a mistake. I can yell at him, berate him, make him feel bad—which I have the *authority* to do—but I have just made a withdrawal from his emotional bank account. Alternatively, I can assume he made the mistake perhaps because he had misunderstood my instructions, or because we did not provide the right training or tools. I can focus my comments on the performance rather than on him as a bad person. He probably went into that meeting thinking he would be fired; he came out of it thinking I'm the best supervisor in the world."

"Because you made a deposit to his emotional bank account?" Sue clarified.

"Exactly. And the point is, all leaders are going to need to ask their followers for some help at some point. A manager needs people to work late one day to meet a customer's deadline. A Rotary club president needs 'All hands on deck' for a volunteerism project. A district governor would like 100% attendance with representation from every club at her district conference . . ."

"Amen to that!" Sue interrupted.

"Those are the times when paybacks occur," Bob continued. "If the person's emotional bank account is empty, he is going to be unable to heed the leader's plea because of 'prior commitments.' But if the leader has made many previous deposits to that emotional bank account, the follower is far more likely to be willing to align his priorities to those of the leader."

"Sue, do you mind if we go back to what you said earlier?" I asked.

"No, of course not, Frank."

"You said you began your presidential year so poorly that you felt nobody in the club wanted to help you meet your goals and objectives. Yet I remember you had a wonderful year—and your club unanimously nominated you for district governor. So how did they change their opinions of you?"

"Because *I* changed my approach," Sue began. "And I have a jigsaw puzzle to thank for it."

The three of us looked at her quizzically, uttering a collective, "Huh?"

"My niece was visiting me, and she loves doing jigsaw puzzles. The last time she had been at my home, we started a new puzzle. It was wonderful, with colorful tropical birds and exotic animals. But on this occasion, almost two months into my presidential year, we could not find the lid—you know, the part with the picture of how the finished puzzle looks. We tried and tried, attaching pieces of the puzzle that we thought might connect—but we got nowhere. Emily went from excited anticipated to outright annoyance. 'How can you expect me to put this together if you can't give me the picture?' she asked.

"That night as I lay in bed reflecting on her disappointment, I had a revelation: my club members were thinking the same thing! I had given them the assignment of meeting my goals and expectations—but without giving them the completed picture. How could I expect them to recruit new members if I hadn't told them why that was important for the club? How could I expect people to give $1,000 each so we could be a 100% Paul Harris Fellow club if I had not shown them the good that this would do?

"So the next week, I cancelled our scheduled speaker and made our meeting a club assembly. I spurned the podium, choosing instead to arrange the tables in a semi-circle and then sat on a stool in the center. I asked the members to forgive me for my insensitivity and asked if we could pretend it was July 1st again. I began by sharing a piece of the big picture of Rotary each week, and then tied the significance of our club goals to that bigger picture. The atmosphere changed almost immediately and we either met or exceeded every goal I had set. It took me a while to realize this, but thanks to little Emily, I learned that if I as a leader of the team do not have the picture, and have not communicated my vision for what the picture looks like to my team members, then I will never be able to complete the puzzle."

"Tell them what we gave you when your year ended," said Bob, grinning.

Sue thought for a moment, and then broke into a broad smile. "Oh, yes! The club presented me with the world's biggest jigsaw puzzle. *Twenty-four thousand pieces!* Do you know how many times I burned the midnight oil trying to put that thing together?"

"Sue," Duncan asked. "How did you win over those team

members who had not been particularly enthusiastic about your ideas?"

"First, I instituted a practice where I sat with different members at each week's meeting. During the meal, I tried to get to know them and learn more about their individual interests and motivations. Then I asked open questions. If I stand before a group and say something like, 'I think we should try X. What do you think?' the result would be mostly blank stares and a few nodding heads. But I have no idea what they *really* think about my idea. I *believe* I have attained agreement, but what I really have is *groupthink*. So when I had my second start, I began asking *open* questions: questions that cannot be answered with a nod and a grunt. I would say something like, 'Jerry, what are the things that stand in the way of meeting this goal?' or, 'Jennifer, what will be the public's perception of our club if we succeed at this project?'"

"I hate to cut this short," I said, looking at my watch, "but I have a conference call coming in from my office in Mexico City in 15 minutes. I have been taking notes as you all spoke, and it seems that communications skills are really critical to effective leadership. I wrote down that good leaders give consistent, encouraging communications through all levels of the organization, and that to be effective as the messenger, you need to know what motivates the audience. What were your main take-away points?"

"The jig-saw puzzle," said Sue. "Every great communicator in history has had the wisdom and ability to first paint a word picture of the vision he wanted the audience to see. The pieces of the puzzle are worthless without knowing what you're working toward."

"I would like to add something," said Duncan. "I agree with Sue's point. But when she referred to 'every great communicator in history,' we think of great *speakers*. You know, JFK, Churchill, Mandela, Martin Luther King. While I agree they were eloquent speakers and great leaders, it was, to all of us here today, *one-way* communication. They spoke; we listened. But leadership skills for us requires two-way communications. I have known hundreds of people who were frustrated in their jobs because they felt their boss never really listened to them. So I would like to add that it is just as important to be a good listener as it is to be an eloquent speaker."

"Good point, Duncan," I said. "And how can we be better listeners?"

Duncan was ready. "With active listening skills. First, you should eliminate distractions. If someone needs to talk to you, turn off your mobile phone and radio, turn away from your computer screen and clear your desktop. Next is eye contact. That is the most effective way of sending a message to the speaker that you are paying attention to them. Use non-verbal cues, such as nodding or note taking. This signals that you are paying attention. Finally, paraphrase in your own words what you think the speaker's message was. Something like, 'So what I hear you saying, Peter, is that if we asked each member to bring in one non-perishable food item to the first meeting of each month, we could donate one ton of food to the homeless shelter in a year. Is that right?'"

"Excellent!" Bob exclaimed. "Just last week I had a problem where I *thought* I had understood what somebody told me, but the whole issue blew up because I had *assumed* I knew what they meant. As it turned out, she had meant one thing and I thought she meant something completely different—and I could have discovered that if I had taken the time in the beginning to truly understand what she was saying."

"May I just interject one problem," Sue asked. "Maybe this is because I am a woman, but I have a real problem maintaining eye contact. I know it's important, but I've talked to other women who share my discomfort with staring into a man's eyes. Any tips on how to make this easier for us?"

"Actually, I do," said Duncan. "You are feeling uncomfortable because you are literally looking into the other man's eyes. But try this. Instead of looking into my eyes, focus your stare right here . . ." He pointed to the top of his nose, exactly at the midpoint between his eyes. Sue complied with his instructions. "Now, how does that feel?"

"It is not uncomfortable at all!" she exclaimed. "I feel I could stare at that spot for 10 minutes."

"Let me tell you a little secret," Duncan said, conspiratorially. "It appears to *me* that you are looking me directly in the eye. Try it on Frank and Bob."

Sue turned her gaze on each of us for several seconds.

"You are making direct eye contact," I stated.

"Yes, eyeball to eyeball," affirmed Bob.

"That's amazing!" said Sue. "I *swear*, I'm not looking anywhere near your eyeball; I'm staring right there at the bridge of your nose. Thanks, Duncan! I can't wait to start making eye contact with people now."

"You see, my friends," I said, standing up, "developing excellent communication skills is an admirable attribute for effective leaders. The leadership skills we learn as Rotarians, working on projects, serving on committees, and then progressing through leadership positions in the club and district unquestionably make us more effective leaders in our careers. Whether we are in Rotary or the outside world, we can have the most impressive credentials from academia or our profession, but if we cannot clearly convey our message and inspire people to act on it, we are doomed to fail. Sue, Duncan, Bob: I will see you in 45 minutes."

What you need to know

✓ The responsibility for ensuring communications have been understood belongs to the leader.

✓ Improve your chances of communications success by focusing on topics of interest to the listener.

✓ The best communicators know the interests of their audience.

✓ Remember the three interlocking circles: *Your values, The Customer's values,* and *Our organization's values* that are interlocked. The leader communicates best by understanding the correlation between the three sets of values.

✓ Remember Covey's admonition: *Seek first to understand before you seek to be understood.*

✓ Improve you communications ability by understanding the different personality types and direct your communications in a "user friendly" style to each type.

✓ Leaders who use persuasion usually create more loyal, enthusiastic teams than those who use authoritarian communications.

✓ Remember to constantly try to make deposits to your team members' emotional bank accounts.

✓ If you can't show your team the picture you're trying to achieve, how are they supposed to put it all together? (The jigsaw analogy)

✓ Effective leaders are good at two-way communications.

✓ Active listening skills:
  - Eliminate distractions
  - Maintain eye contact
  - Use non-verbal cues, such as nodding, smiling, note-taking.
  - Paraphrase back in your own words your understanding of the other person's point.

*"You do not lead
by hitting people over
the head – that's assault,
not leadership."*

President Dwight D. Eisenhower

CHAPTER 5

Towards Unconscious Competence

"When the mind is expanded, it never goes back to its original form."
– Oliver Wendell Holmes

"He's a blithering incompetent, in my opinion. Oh, hello again, Frank." Sue was speaking in an animated fashion as I returned to the group.

"I hope you are not referring to me," I said.

"No, of course not," she said. "I was talking about the waiter. Duncan asked him for mineral water without ice. He came back three times with the wrong thing. We're talking *water* here, Frank! So after almost 20 minutes of waiting, Duncan just walked across the lobby to the gift shop and bought a bottle of Perrier, and now he has his mineral water without ice."

"I can see how frustrating it must be for Duncan," I said. "But it must not be much fun for the waiter, either. And can you imagine what his supervisor would be feeling if he or she knew about this situation? Another major role of a leader is to constantly improve his or her own competency, while increasing the skill sets of those who report to them.

"Yes, it is easy to find fault with a waiter who can't get an order for a glass of water correct, but we need to look beyond the consequence and try to discover the cause. Only then can we introduce changes to assure the problem won't occur again and again. For example, is it a training issue? Or could staffing be a contributory cause . . . you know, three waiters were scheduled to work this afternoon but two of them didn't show up? Or perhaps it could be a logistics issue: the mineral water was in a store room somewhere to which the waiter had no access. I am not excusing the waiter; I am just explaining that poor performance is sometimes caused by issues that are not immediately apparent. Do you know about the four stages of capability?"

My three friends shook their heads indicating they were not familiar with this key psychological concept.

"There are generally considered to be four stages of skill that progress from incompetence to proficiency:

1. Unconscious incompetence is where the individual neither understands nor knows how to do something, nor recognizes the deficit or has a desire to address it.
2. Conscious incompetence is when the individual does not understand or know how to do something, he or she does recognize the deficit, without yet addressing it.
3. Conscious competence is where the individual understands or knows how to do something. However, demonstrating the skill or knowledge requires a great deal of consciousness or concentration.
4. Unconscious competence is when the individual has had so much practice with a skill that it becomes "second nature" and can be performed easily (often without

concentrating too deeply). He or she can also teach it to others."

"So it's like a continuum of competence?" Duncan queried.

"Exactly!" I affirmed. "That's a good way of putting it. And the leader's goal is to move himself—and his people— ever further along that continuum toward being the most competent they can be at whatever they do. Now, why is that important?"

"So that Duncan can get what he wants, the first time he orders it?" suggested Bob. Sue playfully reached over and slapped Bob on the arm.

"Of course, in some situations, that is essentially true," I continued. "Having the confidence to know your people will deliver excellent customer care is certainly a reason to strive for excellence. But let me suggest another: good leaders learn to delegate, so the more competent your team members are, the better the job they will do. That reduces your stress level, increases the team member's self esteem and confidence, and improves the likelihood of meeting your objectives."

"Frank, I am a techie guy who is used to doing things myself," Bob admitted. "You've all heard the admonition, *If you want it done right, do it yourself.* Now that I'm going into management, I have to learn to do things differently. In your opinion, what tasks should a manager delegate?"

"Bob, remember how you have accomplished things as a Rotary club president?" I began. "You delegated many of the assignments and tasks—and you will do the same in your business leadership role. We are interdependent; it is impossible to achieve optimal results without enlisting the help of others on your team. You should delegate anything they can do better than you, faster than you, as well as you, or at a lower cost to the company. You should also delegate anything that could help with the subordinate's development along their own career path."

"That doesn't leave much, Frank!" Sue declared. "Is there anything left? Is there anything we *shouldn't* delegate?"

"Yes," I answered. "You should not delegate tasks that by policy or regulation are your responsibility. Nor should you delegate anything that is confidential or a duty that would abdicate your own authority."

"I believe one way we move along that proficiency continuum is to never stop learning," Duncan volunteered. "For 40 years, I made it a practice of taking at least one continuing education course every three months. I looked at the people we tend to consider consummate professionals: airline pilots, doctors, lawyers, accountants, and learned that they are required to take dozens of continuing professional education hours every year. So I thought to myself, 'If they need to continually sharpen their skills, why shouldn't I?'"

"What sort of courses did you take?" asked Bob.

"I broke them into two categories, which I deemed *hard skills* and *soft skills*. Hard skills were the technical knowledge I needed to know. In the early years, most of the courses fell into this category because I wanted to know everything I could about our products and services. Then as I began moving into supervisory positions, I realized I needed to hone my soft skills. These included the traits that helped me understand my people and how to be a more effective leader."

"Is one category more important than the other?" Bob queried.

"No," said Duncan, flatly. "They are equally important. If you have a manager with awesome technical expertise but who has poor people skills, he won't be successful. And if you have a manager whom the team absolutely loves, but he doesn't know how to train them in the technical skills, he cannot succeed, either. People want a leader that knows more than they do, and also one who demonstrates the people skills that motivate them to perform. The best leaders are those who awaken in their followers a burning desire to themselves think and act as leaders personifying excellence in everything they think, say, and do."

"Duncan has used his career at DuPro in these analogies," Sue observed. "But do you think they also apply in a volunteer position, for example to me as incoming district governor, or to Bob as a club president?"

"I absolutely do," I said. "Why do you think Rotary International spends millions of dollars bringing every district governor-nominee in the world for intensive training at the International Assembly every year? That governor is to be the representative of RI for his or her entire district and it is critically important that every club president and indeed, every Rotarian in the entire district will be able to get accurate information about Rotary's programs and practices from that governor. RI needs reports completed each month, and it cannot have 530 governors sending them in different ways, so it teaches governors-nominee what Duncan called the 'hard' skills. Rotary International recognizes that if the 33,000 clubs and 1.2 million Rotarians are going to learn about its many programs and be motivated to become actively involved in them, the district governor will be the best person to carry the message. So they learn the intricate details of these programs at the International Assembly, too. Then the planners arrange for several round-table discussion groups from experienced past RI officers—people who have probably experienced every situation this incoming class of governors will ever face—and they pass on advice on the soft skills, the interpersonal part of their job. So by the time they leave, they have been given the tools to be effective leaders in their districts—and to train others, such as district officers and club presidents—to lead their people also."

"Is it difficult to manage people who are volunteers?" asked Sue. "I mean, I have already heard some people say, 'She can't tell me what to do. I don't work for her; I'm a volunteer.'"

"It is not *difficult* to oversee volunteers," I said. "But it is different. Organizations have different frameworks, or styles. For example, in Mexico, as in many countries, I see many companies with the autocratic style, where the leader has executive authority and subordinates are oriented toward obediently following the leader's orders. But in Rotary—or any volunteer group, such as Duncan's Red Cross chapter—I suggest what we call the collegial style. This model follows a more collaborative approach, where the leader uses encouragement and motivation to develop more of a self-directed team. With the autocratic style, employees are rewarded with a pay check and job security; rewards are given out by the boss. But do you remember the Hierarchy of Needs that was developed by Abraham Maslow?"

"Sure," said Duncan. "That's where he stated every human being is motivated by certain needs, such as food, shelter, safety, self esteem, and so on."

"That's right," I said. "Maslow said that people are not motivated by higher-level rewards unless their lower-level needs have already been met. The top level of Maslow's hierarchy is what he called *self-actualization needs*, meaning the need to make a difference. Let me illustrate this. If you asked a homeless man sleeping on a heating vent in the winter he would like you to name the college library after him, he would not be motivated by this 'reward.' Why?"

"Because he had not yet met his lower-level needs," said Sue. "He would not consider that a reward at all; but he *would* be motivated by a hot meal, a blanket, a safe place to sleep."

"Precisely," I replied. "Now, let's go to the people you left behind in your district this week. I suspect they don't have to worry about finding a meal or a place to sleep tonight. They already are successful and have lots of friends, so they are at the top level of Maslow's pyramid: self actualization. This is important, because we know that one way we can motivate them is by linking what we want them to do with their perception that they will be making a difference."

"I'd like to add something here," Duncan interjected. "I have found that another way to get top performance is to match your people with the jobs they are best suited for. As leadership guru John Maxwell says, 'Don't send your ducks to eagle school.' I know this sounds obvious, but managers make this mistake all the time. I've seen them take top salespeople at DuPro and make them sales managers—a position that requires entirely different skill sets. It's the same in Rotary: in my own club, I've seen the president appoint someone to a position because she didn't want to make him feel left out, but he failed miserably and ultimately left the club because he felt like he had let us down. And it was all because she was trying to get somebody to do something he hated doing. She sent a duck to eagle school."

"I'd like to make an observation," said Sue. "We have spent a lot of time talking about managing others, but in my experience, the toughest person to manage is myself. I used to have difficulty being on time for meetings and being organized. The year I served as club president really helped me, though. It forced me to plan ahead, set goals, and manage time better. I found it easy to transfer the leadership and self-management skills I developed in Rotary into my business life after that."

"What caused that?" I asked.

"I think it was a case of necessity. I suddenly realized that it was up to me to make it a good year. I didn't see my role so much as trainer of our members as mentor. I already told you how I invested a lot of time trying to discover what motivated each person to be a Rotarian, and then I encouraged them to set one goal that helped our club grow in their own area of interest—and I became their coach, always providing the resources and encouragement to reach those goals."

"When I was Rotary International president, I was in a little different position," I explained. "Unlike you, Sue, I was expected to fall within the structure of this multinational organization that had been doing things *their way* for many years. To some career employees at Rotary headquarters, I was just the temporary custodian of the President's office on the 18th floor. I may have had the title, but they were the people who ran things—at least, that was the perception of some of them. Of course, I knew I would only be in that position for a year, and I was not so presumptuous as to believe I had all the answers. But this was *my* presidency and I wanted to leave my legacy for Rotary, so while I listened to everybody, I knew I had to keep my eye on the prize. Sometimes, we wanted to accomplish something that seemed impossible. The people wanted to do it, but the organization got in the way. In such cases, it is easier to remove the barriers than it is to get people to change.

"The same thing is true in the private sector. We all know how hard it is to make people change their attitudes and beliefs. So why not change the structure that is causing barriers to performance. We've done that in Rotary: we changed attendance requirements, we created eClubs, and some clubs keep Rotary affordable by eliminating the high cost of meals. The result is that we removed the attendance excuse some members had, and everybody benefitted. I know of a Rotarian whose job was making him travel out of the country more than 150 days a year. He was a great Rotarian; he just could not meet the attendance requirements. So his club president proposed, and the board of directors approved, an exception wherein they would still consider him a full member, and he only had to pay on a per-meal basis when he could attend their meetings. They removed the barrier, kept a good member—and one who went on to donate more than $50,000 to The Rotary Foundation. You see, an autocratic leader might well have adopted the stance *You're not meeting the attendance standards; you're out!* But what good would that have done?"

"That's a good lesson," Sue observed. "It illustrates that while some rules are important, others are not inviolable. I guess I need to remember to keep my focus on the people and the ultimate outcomes and not to get hung up on legalisms, and to adapt to changing times. People do respond to the trust and confidence you place in them, don't they?"

"Absolutely," I agreed. "It all boils down to common sense and Rotary has always adapted with changing times. And don't lose sight of what we are discussing here: leadership. By showing your people that you trust them, have confidence in them, and want them to be a part of your team, you are sending signals of what your own character is, what your values are. And as we've already agreed, two of the most important traits of a leader are good character and trustworthiness."

"This has been a good discussion," said Bob. "I used to think management . . . *leadership* . . . was something easily definable. But what I am hearing is that it isn't something that comes out of a box. It is not something you *reach*; it is a continuous journey. Before we go on to the next topic, I need to run over to the gift shop and buy another notepad."

What you need to know

✓ Look beyond the performance problem and ask what might have caused it.

✓ Focus on the performance, not on the person.

✓ Criticise constructively

✓ The 4 stages of the competence continuum are:
  • Unconscious incompetence
  • Conscious incompetence
  • Conscious competence
  • Unconscious competence.

✓ Good leaders delegate whenever possible.

✓ Commit to lifelong learning in both hard skills and soft skills.

✓ Give people assignments that match their interests and skill sets.

✓ Good performance should be rewarded—but to make your reward meaningful, you first need to discover what motivates your people.

✓ The most difficult person to manage is often yourself.

✓ Sometimes it is easier to remove the barriers or change the organization's structure than to change people's attitudes and behaviors.

"I do not want the peace
that passeth understanding;
I want the understanding
which bringeth peace."

Helen Keller

CHAPTER 6

Words of Wisdom

"As irrigators lead the water where they want,
As archers make their arrows straight,
As carpenters carve the wood,
The wise shape their minds."
– The Dhammapada[3]

Bob had barely sat down with his newly acquired notebook when Sue asked a question. "Frank, you mentioned that wisdom is an essential attribute of true leaders. How so? When you hear the word *wisdom*, what do you think of?"

I pondered her question for an easy definition and then began: "I think the first thing a leader should ask is three questions:

1. Where have we come from?
2. What are we doing here? and,
3. Where are we going from here?

Now, as to the real definition of 'wisdom,' I suppose that can only be delivered by observers long after the person has

---

[3] Anthology of Buddhist literature

made his or her decisions. Sometimes, we make a decision or state an opinion that seems wise at the time, but later it seems less so."

"Yes, one of my favorite quotes was made by Thomas Watson, head of IBM, who in 1943 said, 'I think there is a world market for about five computers,'" said Bob. "I have his quote framed and hanging above my desk."

We laughed, and then Duncan spoke: "On the same subject, you all know how much I enjoy military history. Well, one of my favorite quotes—which certainly addresses a leader's wisdom—was made by Napoleon Bonaparte, who said, 'I tell you Wellington is a bad general, the English are bad soldiers; we will settle the matter by lunch time.' Napoleon uttered those words at breakfast with his generals on the morning before the Battle of Waterloo."

"You have both proven my point," I continued. "Wisdom, or discernment, is best viewed after the fact over a long time period. Some words and phrases go into and out of vogue: think of *"Duh!," "proactive," "paradigm shift," "cool!,"* and so on. Yet wisdom is never out of favor. I travel a lot, and I can tell you that no matter the country or the culture or the type of industry or religious faith of the people I meet, wisdom is a recurring and always-fashionable attribute of their leaders. But those on our team—we've been calling them *followers* today—will look to us for wisdom in how we address issues that present themselves in the present. So how can we be perceived as discerning leaders?"

"Having just gone through the intensive International Assembly governor's training course, I think my knowledge will increase my competence, and that should help me make wiser decisions," said Sue.

"So are you saying that *experience* leads to wisdom?" I asked.

"Interesting question," Duncan surmised. "On the one hand, yes, experience can lead to one's making wise decisions. I am sure the past RI officers used their many years of experience to demonstrate their leadership skills to Sue and her other incoming district governors, for example. But I have seen politicians and people in the private sector with boatloads of experience who made some of the worst decisions imaginable. So I suppose I would answer that experience *can* lead to wisdom, but it is not a guarantee. I am thinking back to some of the wisest people I have ever worked with and I would include experience, but also modesty, composure, and good communications skills to the list of essential ingredients of the definition of wisdom.

"So if we can stay with the example of Sue and her new-found knowledge she learned at the International Assembly, is it fair to say that she came away from the conference with *knowledge*, but the knowledge could emerge as wisdom when Sue combines her knowledge with other attributes such as patience, integrity, and good communications?"

"I agree with that," said Bob. "I recently got some advice from my boss—the one I told you has been mentoring me. He gently pointed out to me that I had a tendency to interrupt people when they were asking me questions by jumping in with the answer. I did that because I guess I had the technical skills that earned me the promotion. But he showed me that sometimes by interrupting the questioner, I had not heard what their *real* concern was. So he taught me to wait until they had stopped talking, and then wait five seconds before beginning my answer. He said this first avoids an interruption if they had not finished, and second, the five seconds makes me look as if I am really thinking about their question rather than making a knee-jerk response."

"Speaking as the analytical person in the group," said Duncan, "I believe it is important how we respond to questions. We can reply with information, in which case we are simply giving them facts. But to answer with wisdom goes further. It adds our values, judgment, and character to the facts. But remember—and I am giving this advice as an engineer who normally relies on left-brain. Data is not information, information is not knowledge, knowledge is not understanding, and understanding is not wisdom."

"Boy, I'm glad I have a notebook to write that one down," said Bob.

"Can we agree that knowledge is not wisdom, but wisdom comes from the correct use of knowledge?" I asked.

"I agree with that," said Sue. Duncan and Bob both nodded their assent.

"So we might perceive a wise person as brilliant, even though they might not be academically accomplished," said Bob, looking at his notes. You could have brains without having wisdom, but a person with wisdom understands what is needed."

"I'd like to add to that thought," I continued. "Just because we know something does not make us wise, neither is being *right* synonymous with wisdom. I had a friend who once had an argument with a fellow club member and he resigned on the spot. There was no question in my mind he was on right side of the disagreement, but he acted too brashly. Rotary lost a darned good member, but he was so obsessed with having been right that he could not back down and rejoin the club—and he regrets not being a Rotarian to this day. Now what do you think a true leader should have done in that case?" I asked.

"I think the member should have picked his battles," said Sue. "He should have thought, 'I have the right to be upset with this other guy, but the long-term consequences of my resignation are not worth the temporary satisfaction I might have from doing it.'"

"And the club president or anybody with wisdom in the club should have brought the two of them together and acted as a peacemaker," added Bob.

"One of the things I learned the year I was club president was that when we are dealing with people, we must often set logic aside," Sue interjected. "Some people think, act, and speak mainly from emotions; they have prejudices, pride and vanity that get in the way of rational thought. Too many times, egos and arrogance take over, and when that happens, everybody loses. The innocent bystanders—the employees, customers, or, in this cases, the other club members feel very uncomfortable when they see it, the person at the receiving end of egotistical behavior feels angry, and the person dishing it out loses face with everybody."

I could see from the nodding heads that Sue was not the only one who had witnessed self-serving brashness.

"The thing about leadership is that your followers have to buy in to what you're doing. If they think you are hot-headed or acting for your own egotistical reasons, you've lost them," I added.

"So a wise person knows when to keep his mouth shut," Bob summarized.

"As always, Bob gets straight to the point," said Sue.

"My dad used to tell us, 'God gave you one mouth and two ears; use them in the same proportion.'"

"Let me add another thought," I said. "My friend David Linett is an accomplished attorney who graduated from Harvard Law School. He became an RI Director and was the founder of the Rotary Leadership Institute, which teaches leadership skills to Rotarians in 200 districts around the world. Dave told me that at Harvard Law School they taught students how to analyze legal cases; how to *think* like a lawyer. 'If you can do that,' he told me, 'you can always learn the mechanics of how to write a brief or how to do what lawyers do.' I know we just spent quite a while talking about the importance of being competent in your job, but what Dave Linett says is also true, the person with wisdom knows how to *think* like a leader."

Sue put down her pen and with a pained expression looked me directly in the eye. "Frank, I *think* I have wisdom—but I suppose everybody feels that way about themselves. I know the people in my district like me, and I want to be successful as their governor next year. But after going through the governor's training program I feel overwhelmed—like the kid in the proverbial candy store. There are so many programs and projects I would like us to do, plus I want to increase membership, Rotary Foundation giving, maybe add some new clubs . . . I don't know where to start! I only have one year as governor; I don't feel I am demonstrating wisdom at all! What should I do?"

"What you are feeling is not at all unusual, Sue," I answered, trying to sound reassuring. You *are* a leader, a *wise* leader. And one of my top ten attributes for leaders is that they have focus. Since you brought it up, why don't we talk about that now."

What you need to know

✓ The first three questions every leader asks:
   1. Where have we come from?
   2. What are we doing here?
   3. Where are we going from here?

✓ Experience complements, but does not necessarily lead to wisdom.

✓ "Data is not information, information is not knowledge, knowledge is not understanding, and understanding is not wisdom."

✓ Being *right* is not synonymous with wisdom.

"Give me a stock clerk with a goal and I'll give you a man who will make history. But give me a man with no goals and I'll give you a stock clerk."

J. C. Penney, Department store magnate and Rotarian

CHAPTER 7

Keep your Eyes on the Prize

"Keep your mind on the main thing."
– John C. Maxwell, *Leadership Gold*

"Let's start with an irrefutable statement: *you can't do everything*," I told Sue. " I empathize with you. You have a hundred ideas you would like to implement next year, and why? Perhaps for your own ego, but knowing you, it's more likely because you really believe you would improve the lives of countless needy people *and* you would introduce some exciting programs to your district. I went through the same process before I became Rotary International president. But if you try to accomplish too much, you risk achieving poor results in everything—and burning out your volunteers.

"I suggest you write down everything you think you could realistically accomplish in your district. Then pare down the list to a few that are doable. Of those, ask yourself, 'What is the main thing?'"

"What do you mean *the main thing*?" asked Bob.

"It is the most important essential that simply must be accomplished. It is your *raison d'etre*: your reason for being," I explained. "It's 10 minutes before the shops close and you need to go to the office supply store to buy a new printer cartridge; you need an oil change that is way overdue, and tomorrow is your wife's birthday and you have not yet bought her a card. Which store do you head towards?"

"Well . . . are the printer cartridges on sale today?" asked Bob with an impish look.

Sue reached over and slapped him. "You'd better *not* hesitate with the answer to that question, Bob!"

"I get it!" said Bob, dodging Sue's hand. "Obviously, taking care of my wife is more important than any other task before me at that moment. So I do the one main thing—buying her a birthday card—and relegate the other assignments to somebody else, or I do them the next day."

"That's right, Bob," I agreed. "You get an A for the course so far. So as leaders, we must recognize we are accountable to others, such as our bosses, our companies, our customers, our club members, our district governor for accomplishing the main thing. If you don't know what the main thing is, perhaps you are not ready for leadership. The easiest way to find out is to ask the person to whom you report.

"Now, one of the biggest reasons we feel stressed, and fail to meet our goals, is that we don't manage our time very well. We respond to interruptions, time wasters, and things that seem urgent—yet they are not important. I suggest you make a list of everything you need to accomplish at the beginning of the year. Don't prioritize it or think too much about what you are writing down at that moment; just brainstorm and get items on your list. When you think you are finished, go back over the list and put an A, B, or C beside each item. A items are *must do* things. You will have failed in your leadership role if you have not completed them. B items are *should do* tasks: you really would like to accomplish some or all of these, but if you do not, you will not be considered a failure. Finally, C items are *would like to do* things. It would be nice if you had time to get them done, but it will not really affect your career or your leadership position if you do not.

"Let me pick on Sue this time. Submitting the paperwork to The Rotary Foundation for a matching grant is an A item, because if she doesn't get it in by the deadline, her district will not be able to fund its project for providing clean water to a country in Africa. Growing district-wide membership by 10 percent net is a wonderful goal, but if it is not reached, Sue will not have failed as your governor. It is certainly important, but not an essential objective— so we'll categorize that as a B task. Finally, Sue loves to sing, and she noted at the international assembly that many Rotary clubs sing during their meetings. She thinks that would be a nice addition to club fellowship—but it would be a C item, because if some clubs vehemently object to her suggestion, it is not worth fighting over. Does that make sense?"

"Yes, it does," said Duncan. "Now how far out do you make this list?"

"It depends," I replied. "For my business, or my career, I might set a five- or 10-year time horizon. Obviously, in Rotary, most offices are only held for one year, so I would make it a 12-month objective. But I break my goals down into daily components."

"You know, Frank, this is a very timely discussion. My boss has asked me to provide him with my goals for the next three years and one year, and I wasn't even clear about how to define 'goals'; it is one of those business words that is bandied around freely. How do you define a goal?"

"I find it easy to use acronyms to remember things," I began. "And goals should be SMART. They should be specific, measurable, achievable, relevant, and time-framed. You see, many people say they have set a goal, but it is really just a whim, a wish. First, to be a real goal, you must write it down. If it isn't in writing, it is not a goal. Now, let me pick on Duncan. Let's say Duncan wakes up one day, looks in the mirror, and says, 'Oh my! I am so overweight. I really need to lose weight.' Is that a goal?"

"Sure," said Bob.

"What do you think?" I said, directing my question at Sue and Duncan.

"It may be the truth, but it is not a goal," Duncan answered.

"Why not?" I asked.

"Because it wasn't written down," Sue suggested.

"That's part of it," I said. "But use the SMART acronym. Is 'I really need to lose weight' *specific*?"

"No."

"Is it *measurable*?"

"Not really."

"Is it *achievable, relevant* and *time-framed*?"

"It was none of those," Bob admitted.

"Good," I continued. "Now, help Duncan set a SMART goal."

"I want to lose 25 pounds—that's specific; by December 31st this year," said Duncan.

"Excellent!" I said. "Twenty-five pounds is specific, he can weigh himself each week to see how he is progressing toward his goal—so it is measurable; he has seven months to lose 25 pounds, so that is certainly achievable and relevant, and he framed the goal with a date so he will be able to count back from December 31st to today and set mini weekly and monthly goals to check his progress toward attaining his written ultimate objective. That is a SMART goal."

"So I should set my goals for, say, a three-year time horizon and then break that down into sub-goals for what has to be accomplished this year to move toward that goal, and then could even break this year's objectives down into monthly or even weekly goals?" asked Bob.

"Absolutely!" I affirmed. "Why would you wait until three years from now to see how you are doing? I may have mentioned my friend who sells real estate. He sets a one-year goal, then, knowing his average commission, breaks it down into a *daily* goal. He knows he has to make so-many telephone calls each day and obtain so-many listings each week. Every month, he checks his year-to-date progress with his goal. If the market has changed and his average sales price has declined, he knows his year-end commission will also be below target, so he increases the number of daily calls he makes and that invariably increases the number of listings he earns. So there are three parts of effective goal setting: first, put them in writing; second, use SMART goals, and third, monitor your progress toward them and make adjustments as necessary."

"I am a private pilot," said Duncan. "Before I get into the cockpit, I plan my route and check the weather. I might learn that with the winds coming from, say, 330° at five knots, I need to maintain a heading of 270° to reach my destination in two hours. But half an hour after takeoff, I might discover

I have drifted to the south of my course. That is because the *actual* winds are now coming from 340° at 10 knots. So I need to adjust my heading. Perhaps now I must actually head 275° and the stronger headwinds will take me an extra 10 minutes to reach my destination. It is absolutely essential that pilots use a checklist and constantly monitor their progress and make adjustments because the *real* weather and wind conditions are rarely exactly what the forecasters tell us to expect."

"That's a great analogy," said Sue. "As you were explaining it, I was thinking how that parallels what we must face as leaders in business—or in Rotary. Even when we do set our course, we seldom find the real world to be exactly as we anticipated it, and to succeed in our mission, we need to know if we are going off course and to make adjustments without getting upset about the continual corrections."

"I hate to be negative," said Bob, "but what I worry about is setting a goal and then failing. That would make me look terrible to both my team members and my boss. I bet a lot of people never set goals—or at least, they don't set very challenging goals—because of the fear of failure"

"I think that is true," said Duncan. "How do you respond to that, Frank?"

"A lot of that goes back to your self esteem," I said. "It is easy to let yourself be dragged down by negative self-talk. But I realize the more successful I am, the more failures I will have. Failure is like fertilizer; it stinks. But the more I have the more I grow. Plato once said, 'The first and best victory is to conquer one's self.' The biggest reason leaders fail to achieve their objectives is that they fail to plan and then let themselves believe they are failures. If Bob sets a goal for a 10 percent increase in his club membership this year and they only increase by eight percent, is he a failure? If Sue sets her heart on getting $150,000 in donations to The Rotary Foundation next year but only collects $125,000, is she a failure? *No!* Of course not! They have fallen short of some tangible goals, but they are not failures. However, if they do as Duncan suggested in his flight plan analogy and set SMART goals and then constantly monitor their progress towards their goals, making adjustments along the way—and if they continually communicate the need to the stakeholders to participate in those goals—they can turn things around even when it sometimes seems the goal is elusive. Just make sure you never take your eyes off the prize.

"I remember hearing a story once of a commissioned salesperson whose manager asked for his most important goal. The young salesman said it was to own a Rolls-Royce. So the sales manager went to the Rolls-Royce dealership and picked up several brochures of these magnificent cars. He pasted one on the salesman's desk, one next to his telephone, one of the restroom wall, one on the dashboard of his car, and told the young guy to paste the rest all around his home, which he did—including one that he pasted on the ceiling above his bed. The first thing he saw in the morning, the last thing before he closed his eyes at night, and all throughout the day—was his dream car. He then calculated how many sales he would need to buy a Rolls-Royce by the end of his second year. Twenty-three months after he began working, he walked into the dealership and bought a Rolls-Royce."

"I don't necessarily agree with his priorities," said Duncan. "A goal like that conflicts with my idea of stewardship, but I can see how, as Frank said, keeping his eyes on what to this young man was the ultimate goal motivated him to strive toward it with every waking moment."

"Frank, Duncan made me think of a question," said Sue. "Perhaps it's the maternal instinct in me, but I think I would have told this 23-year-old kid he was crazy having a goal of spending almost $200,000 on a car. Yet I realize as leaders, we ourselves often face criticism for what we are trying to accomplish. That can be downright debilitating sometimes. How do you keep your spirits up when you experience resistance to your plans?"

I thought back to my terms as club president, district governor, RI Director, and RI President and while all these positions brought me untold moments of happiness as I sought to serve the Rotarians of the world, I also experienced criticism. "This is not an easy issue to address," I began. "First, let me say that leaders need to expect some criticism. Criticism itself is not necessarily a bad thing if it helps you plan better and end up with better results. So during your preparations you should take the skeptic's position and ask yourself, 'Why *shouldn't* we do this? What is the downside of this idea? What would the most negative person in my department find wrong with this?' None of us has the franchise on brilliance, so it can be helpful to anticipate what others might find troubling with your presentation or your ideas. I read recently: 'Don't mind criticism. If it is untrue, disregard it; if it is unfair, keep from irritation; if it is ignorant, smile; if it is justified, it is not criticism—learn from it.' But if you do encounter a team member whom you just can't seem to motivate, you might want to speak to them privately; explain the importance of your objective, and then seek agreement that if they are not prepared to *help you* achieve it, at least they won't obstruct you."

"I am surprised that somebody of your stature would have been criticized," said Bob. "You were the president of Rotary for the whole world, that's about the most impressive title of anybody I have ever known. If *you* were criticized as our leader, what hope is there for the rest of us to be considered good leaders?"

I smiled. "Bob, having a title doesn't make you a leader. Do you know who Lou Holtz is?"

Before Bob could reply, Duncan smiled and answered. "Oh sure. He is one of the most successful college football coaches in U.S. history. He was head football coach at my alma mater, Notre Dame."

"Correct," I said. "I heard Lou tell the story of his first meeting with Father Hesburgh, then president of Notre Dame, after accepting the position as head coach. Lou said, 'When I became head coach at Notre Dame, Father Hesburgh told me, 'I can give you the title of head coach, but that won't make you the leader of the team. Because titles come from above, but players determine if you are their leader. I asked him, 'What makes you a leader?' He told me, 'You have to have a vision, a plan, you must lead by example, and you have to hold people accountable.'

"That sums up what we have been talking about, doesn't it? You have to have a vision for where you are going and a plan for how you will get there. You need to assign the right people to the right tasks and then hold everybody—starting with yourself—accountable for executing their part of the plan."

"I truly believe that accountability is a huge part of leadership," said Duncan. "I spent more than 40 years in the private sector. I've spent a dozen years in various leadership roles in volunteer organizations, and I also read the newspapers.

I taught my children that they are personally responsible for the consequences of their decisions—and they lived by those rules. Yet we see people resorting to the blame game all the time. Late for work? Just blame the traffic! You spilled hot coffee in your lap because you decided to try and drive a car while holding the cup? Just sue McDonalds! You bought a house you couldn't afford? Blame the mortgage company and default on the loan!"

"Boy, I guess we know where Duncan's hot button is!" said Bob, with a laugh.

"But accountability is an important leadership attribute," I responded. "It is an easy word to define, and yet there are several different dimensions to accountability. Duncan touched on one of them: you hold your kids to a set of behavioral expectations, and reward or punish them based on the results. I know some people who meet every couple of weeks in small accountability groups where they set personal or professional goals and then hold one another accountable for delivering on their promises to the group. Businesses are accountable: to the community, to the environment, to their stockholders and employees."

"I learned a lesson in accountability from my district governor the year I was club president," Sue declared. "When I first received the forms for me to outline my plans and objectives for my presidential year, one of the past presidents told me to just put anything down because nobody ever does anything with them Luckily, I ignored his advice and I spent a lot of time and thought describing my goals for the year. When the governor made his official visit, he examined each objective and asked me how I was going to achieve it, how I was doing so far, and what I was planning to do next. Once a month, he called me for one thing or another, and inevitably he would say something like, 'Now Sue, last month you told me you were going to have a guest night to introduce prospective members to your club.' Did you hold that yet? How did it go? How many prospects are you working on? What can I do to help you meet that goal?' It was a valuable lesson for me, because even though I was a volunteer, he let me know that if I was going to say I would do something, he would hold me accountable for showing I was delivering on that commitment."

"I have a question," said Bob, flipping back through his notebook. "Using your essential leadership skills attributes, wasn't Hitler an effective leader?"

Sue looked aghast at such a suggestion.

"Well, let's look at Bob's question seriously," I said, hoping for the rationale to answer it wisely. Going back to my top ten list, did Hitler have charisma?"

"He sure did," said Duncan. "He had a magnetism that made people believe in him and his sick vision."

"OK then," I continued. "And you have just confirmed he had another leadership trait: vision. Was he a good communicator? I've seen old films of his speeches at places like Nuremburg and he was electrifying. Was he goal oriented, was he passionate about reaching those goals, was he a problem solver?"

"Yes, in the most vile form ever known in human history," said Sue, disgustedly. "He solved the problem by creating concentration camps for his 'problems.'"

"And there you have it," I declared. "Hitler surely had some of the skills required by leaders and I think most people would agree, he was effective to a certain degree. But—and here is the huge *but* that we should underline— Hitler was not a leader by our definition because he did not have the heart of a servant leader. He was self-centered, totally lacking integrity, and was not accountable—he was not accountable to a higher power, nor to the ethical standards we have to our fellow man, nor to the citizens of his country.

"We must hold to account those in power, whether they are politicians, executives, or leaders in the volunteer community. We accept the title and with that comes a responsibility to be transparent and to teach, coach, and motivate those on our team."

What you need to know

✓ You cannot do everything! For optimal results you must involve others. Leaders constantly remind themselves, *What is the main thing?*

✓ Set goals at least a year out, then work backwards to set mini-goals on a monthly, weekly, and daily basis.

✓ Goals must be written down and should be SMART:
  • Specific
  • Measurable
  • Achievable
  • Relevant
  • Time-framed

✓ Have a daily "To Do" list, with each item prioritized with an A, B, or C:
  • A is for "must do" tasks
  • B is for "should do" items
  • C is for "would like to do" things.

✓ Remember the pilot analogy and constantly evaluate where you are relative to reaching your goal, and make frequent adjustments as necessary.

✓ If you fail to make 100% of your goal, you are not a failure.

✓ Before you announce your goal, think like a skeptic: what could go wrong with this plan? Expect criticism; think proactively, and don't take it personally.

✓ Having a title doesn't make you a leader.

✓ Hold yourself—and your people—accountable.

"If I have seen farther than others, it is because I was standing on the shoulder of giants."

Isaac Newton

CHAPTER 8

Servant Leadership

*"The biggest disease today is not leprosy
or tuberculosis, but rather the feeling of being
unwanted, uncared for, and deserted by everybody.
The greatest evil is the lack of love and charity, the
terrible indifference toward one's neighbor."*
– Mother Teresa

"So although he had the *title*, are you saying a head football coach would not be the team's leader unless the players respected him?" Sue asked.

"That's right," I said. "And respect stems from trust. The team members must trust that their leader knows his or her job—we already talked about the need to be proficient—but also that he or she cares about each member of the team. That is why one of my 10 essentials for effective leaders is that they be servant leaders."

"How do you define that?" asked Duncan.

"It is a concept that goes back thousands of years," I explained. "The Chinese sage Lao Tzu back in 600 B.C. wrote of how the greatest leaders forget themselves and focus on developing their followers. Jesus taught his disciples that whoever wants to be great among you must also be your servant. Bob has referred to his boss several times. I don't know whether he intended to make a distinction, but I see a difference between being a leader and being a manager; a boss. The boss uses a hierarchical top-down approach to managing people, whereas servant leaders use a more collegial style that emphasizes trust, cooperation, and empathy. Servant leaders turn the traditional management pyramid upside down.

"I once read a book that advocated the customer comes second! We all know that's ridiculous: the customer must come first, or we go out of business. But the author's hypothesis was that by putting his *employees* first, by creating a workplace that was fun, rewarding, challenging, trusting, and encouraging of their own expectations, they would be so motivated that they would treat every customer with superb service. We normally put the employees at the bottom of the pyramid, then the managers above them, the directors above them and the president at the top. By reversing the order, the employees will likely be happier, more likely to buy in to the leader's agenda, and will ultimately deliver significantly better results than under the traditional model. The objective is not to use one's power that comes with the leadership title, but to seek ways to help each person on the team grow and develop to the best of their abilities. We become their *coach*, trying to find what they do best and then provide them with the tools and encouragement—always cheering them on and rooting for them to succeed."

"Wow!" Sue exclaimed. "If I had had a boss like that, I never would have quit the airline business. My manager was a complete idiot. He never gave any of us credit for our work; in fact, he would take credit for our own ideas when he went to the managers meeting in New York. Nobody trusted him; we hated him."

"The airlines are a perfect example of the best and worst leadership styles," said Duncan. "I used to fly every week, and I swear you could tell from the service you received how well the managers treated the frontline employees. The workers with the big legacy carriers felt cheated and abused by upper management and they delivered service that was typically uncaring and downright sullen. Yet when I flew JetBlue and Southwest—where managers *do* have a servant attitude toward their people—I cannot every remember encountering a rude or indifferent employee. That's because those corporate leaders adopted a culture of empowering their people rather than dominating them. Again, if you will endure the history buff in me, President Calvin Coolidge once said, 'No person was ever honored for what he received. Honor has been the reward for what he gave.' I think that could also apply to a servant leader."

"Speaking of history, I had breakfast with a group of British Rotarians at the International Assembly," Sue recalled. "One of the told an interesting story. Back in Victorian England, the two greatest political rivals were William Gladstone and Benjamin Disraeli. The story goes that a young lady had dinner with both men, on consecutive nights. She was then asked for her opinions of the two famous, powerful political opponents. 'When I sat next to Mr. Gladstone, I thought he was the cleverest man in England,' she said. 'But after sitting next to Mr. Disraeli, I thought I was the cleverest *woman* in England.' I've thought about that vignette many times since I heard it in January, and what it says to me is that I should always try to focus on the other person, rather than try to impress them with me."

"I would consider Gladstone to have demonstrated servant leadership, wouldn't you?" I asked, adding: "He certainly had the title, but he didn't need to use it to make a positive impression on his guest."

"I see servant leadership connected to generosity, to service" said Bob. "And as Rotarians, that certainly shouldn't be a foreign concept for us. One of my favorite quotes was from a poem I picked up while I was working in India. The poet Rabindranath Tagore Bengali—whom Indians call the 'King of poets,' wrote: *I slept and dreamt that life was joy. I awoke and saw that life was service. I acted, and behold, service was joy.*"

"I like that." Duncan added. "I used to think of *service* as something we do for others, an *external* action. But I can see that a servant leader considers service to start at home, so to speak. In my case, I should be devoting more time trying to find how to serve the people who report to me at the Red Cross. I just remembered how we were all asked to read *The One Minute Manager* when it was first published. The part that stayed with me all these years later is that the key to developing people is to catch them doing something right. I think I have forgotten to apply that since I retired."

"And I should try to foster a sense of community with my team at work," said Bob. "It's funny; until now, I would have considered *servant* and *leader* to be complete opposites. But I can see that by applying some of the techniques we have discussed here today: listening skills, empathy, trust, persuasion, and a commitment to helping the employee's development—this can only lead to a really committed, motivated team."

"You're right!" I agreed. "You see, being a servant leader does not imply weakness, it simply takes the focus away from you and your authority and transfers the focus to your people. Look, I attended a wedding recently and the minister used the famous 'love' passage from I Corinthians in his charge to the bride and groom. Of course, we've all heard the passage many times: *Love is patient, love is kind*, and so on. But this time he expanded on the reading to what love *is not* . . . and I believe the same applies to the way servant leaders act. Let's substitute the word 'love' for the word 'leaders,' as we are trying to define them today. How does this sound? *Leaders are patient*—now 'patient' does not mean they will tolerate missed deadlines and poor performance; *Leaders are kind*—they are not pushovers, but they are genuinely nice towards others; *Servant Leaders do not envy, they do not boast, they are not self-seeking nor easily angered.* And then we switch to the positive affirmations: *Leaders always protect, always trust, always hope, always persevere.* Does that make sense?"

"It really does," said Bob.

"Now," I said, holding up my finger to emphasize my point. "Let's make this *really* personal. I want you to imagine how effective you would be as a leader if those who reported to you described you this way: *Bob* is patient, Bob is kind. *Sue* does not envy, Sue does not boast, she is not self-seeking nor easily angered. *Duncan* always protects his people, always trusts, always hopes, always perseveres."

"Frank, that is very powerful," said Sue, still writing. "You have taken the whole concept of servant leadership and made it feel relevant just to me, giving me something to work towards as a personal goal. I so often jump to conclusions and get impatient and angry when people don't do what I asked them to do, so this really helps me."

"I just thought of something," said Bob. "The Four-Way Test also points to servant leadership. When we say . . . no, when we truly *embrace* questions such as 'Is it fair to all concerned?' and 'Will it build goodwill and better friendship?' and 'Will it be beneficial to all concerned?' our focus is on the other person. We are thinking of them rather than ourselves."

"I hadn't thought if that," I admitted. "But you are right. And once again you have just made a direct link between Rotary and leadership. Those who are Rotarians—not members of Rotary clubs, but *Rotarians*—have so many tools to help develop them into excellent leaders. We learn the value of awareness, of listening skills, of compassion. And we see the difference between old-line management skills that use coercion, domination, manipulation and the skills a servant leader employs, such as persuasion, team building and persuasion.

"And servant leadership gives added meaning to what we call Service Above Self in Rotary. Let me add one more thing. I mentioned before that I attended the Institute for Leadership in El Paso, Texas. Jaime Gonzalez, one of the trainers, made a very powerful point that links my point about servant leadership directly with the Object of Rotary—with which every one of us is familiar. He says this concept of servanthood, or service, appears all through our entire reason for being. Listen:

"The object of Rotary is to encourage and foster the ideal of service as a basis of worthy enterprise and, in particular, to encourage and foster:

1. The development of acquaintance as an opportunity for *service*;
2. High ethical standards in business and professions; the recognition of the worthiness of all useful occupations; and the dignifying by each Rotarian of his occupation as an opportunity to *serve* society;
3. The application of the ideal of *service* by every Rotarian to his personal, business and community life;
4. The advancement of international understanding, good will, and peace through a world fellowship of business and professional people united in the ideal of *service*.

"You see, *service* is not an alien concept to Rotarians; we have been practicing it for more than one hundred years!"

What you need to know

✓ Servant Leadership is not *weakness*; it simply takes the focus away from you and your authority and transfers the focus to your people.

✓ Servant leaders put their followers first.

✓ Service Above Self also applies to how a leader treats his direct-reports.

✓ Try to foster a sense of community within your team.

✓ Servant leaders embrace the Four-Way Test in their relationships with their team.

"The pessimist sees difficulty in every opportunity. The optimist sees opportunity in every difficulty."

Winston Churchill

CHAPTER 9

Thinking Positive

*"A successful man is one who can
lay a firm foundation with the bricks
others have thrown at him."*
– David Brinkley

"Frank, I was at a breakfast at the International Assembly, and some past district governors were discussing who were the most popular past presidents and directors of Rotary International. Some names came up time and again as being among the best senior leaders Rotary International ever had. Do you know *why* those people spoke so favorably about them?"

"No, why?" I asked.

"It was because of the passion they have for their message. Whether they are urging people to support PolioPlus, Preventable Blindness, membership development or The Rotary Foundation, it was clear to everybody that those leaders really believe what they say and are committed to the cause."

"Well, Sue," I began. "Firstly, I must correct one impression that you are giving to Bob and Duncan: I am sure *all* past RI Presidents just as committed to Rotary as . . ."

"Excuse me for interrupting, Frank," she interjected. "Please don't think I was being critical or judgmental of the others. All I was doing was passing on what these very experienced people were saying about the *best* leaders, in their view."

"Well, you are right, I suppose," I continued. "Some speakers are more passionate about our organization and everything Rotarians do to make the world a better place, and it is interesting to hear that this is so noticeable. I believe one has to be optimistic about life; look at what the alternative would be! A long time ago, somebody taught me that you aptitude plus your attitude determine your altitude—and I have fervently lived by that maxim ever since.

"People like to follow optimistic leaders. At Devlyn Optical, how would my employees feel if I walked into one of our retail stores and shared with them how worried I was about the economy, and a new discount competitor, and how that community was in decline? How effective would those salespeople be the next time a client walked in? We would lose sales—and probably lose our employees, too. I am not saying a leader should look at the world through rose-colored glasses to the extent that he or she is out of touch with reality, but after setting our goals we need to have the confidence and enthusiasm to truly believe we can reach them. That cheerful self-belief is noticed by our followers and most of them feel a sense of assurance that they, too, can accomplish what you have challenged them to do."

"Do you remember my telling you we interviewed several real estate agents when we decided to sell our last home?" asked Bob. We nodded. "One of the Realtors, who was a very experienced agent, spent a good part of her interview time saying how awful the market was, and how homes like ours were sitting unsold for up to a year. By the time she left, we said to one another, 'If she doesn't believe our house can sell, how in the world is she going to be able to confidently act as our representative to prospective buyers and agents?' The broker we chose seemed really excited about what we had done to our home; she saw distinctive differences between competing properties and ours, and had a certain confidence that seemed infectious."

"My old Girl Scout leader used to tell us, 'Sometimes life will give you lemons, and you can focus on the bitterness or turn them into lemonade.'" said Sue. "I told you earlier about my bad start as club president. I thought about her advice many times during those first few weeks."

"What is important is that you *did* turn them into lemonade," I said. "I am sure some of your club members were observing you to see how you reacted to adversity. By showing them that even when you changed course, you did so with a positive attitude and never showed animosity or ill will, you won them over."

"I have been trying to recall the exact quotation, but it escapes me," Duncan interjected. "But George Bernard Shaw once wrote that true joy in life is when you recognize that you have a purpose. He contrasted that to 'selfish little clots' focused on their ailments and grievances, and reasoned that those were the people who complained that the world does not devote itself to making them happy. I have always thought that although we greet one another with questions such as 'How are you?' the person doesn't really want to hear about it if you are having a day from hell. It's the same when I go into one of the seminars here at the convention. I really don't care to hear the speaker opening with five minutes about how bad his flight connections were yesterday. I would much rather listen to a presenter who is upbeat, enthusiastic, and self-assured."

"I think leaders genuinely believe they can positively shape their lives," Sue declared.

"Let me add one thing," I said. "So far, it seems to me that we have focused our attention on the verbal part of portraying self-confidence. I suggest that we also remember something that is often overlooked: body language. Look at that guy over there. What can you tell about him?"

They all looked across the lobby to a waiter, probably in his mid-twenties, carrying a tray of drinks to a table of six customers.

"I don't have a good impression of him," said Bob. "I don't think he likes his job. He may not even like himself very much."

"Wow! You jumped to quite a conclusion," I replied. "What led you to think that?"

"He is slouching along, almost dragging his feet as he walks," Bob answered.

"And his shirt is hanging out on the left side," Sue observed.

Duncan lowered his voice: "I know this is in vogue with some young people, but I also notice he is unshaven. I think that makes him look shabby. Oh, and look: his shoes are not clean."

As the waiter delivered the drinks, Sue added one more comment: "Look at that, he just gave six guests a drink and he didn't once break a smile and show any enthusiasm to them. I think he hates his job and probably has low self-esteem."

I held up my hand to stop the exercise. "Remind me not to ask you to pass judgment on *me!*" I said. "Here's my point: we don't know anything about that man. He could be highly educated, have a wonderful home life, and be a paragon of virtue—and yet you have the impression that he is an unkempt, miserable loser, with bad attitude toward work and life in general—all because of his body language."

My three friends looked guilty for jumping to their conclusions.

"No, I am not criticizing you," I quickly added. "I am pointing out the importance of body language as part of our whole communications commitment. I met somebody in California who is a jury consultant. Trial attorneys pay her tens of thousands of dollars to determine the likely attitudes of potential jurors for big trials. She told me that even before they open their mouths, she can, with amazing accuracy, know whether that person is lazy or industrious, intelligent or slow, open- or closed-minded—just from observing their body language."

"So you mean all those years of my mother telling me to 'sit up straight' were not wasted?" asked Sue.

"Apparently not," I said. She told me an erect posture indicates the person has intelligence and self-confidence."

"I believe the key to positive thinking is to realize this: *If I believe I can or if I believe I cannot—I am probably right*," I said. "I know that sounds like a cliché, but it is the truth. You need to believe in yourself and have passion for your mission. Rational thinking is when you come up short and say to yourself, 'I didn't accomplish the end result I had hoped for, but here is what I learned from the exercise…' Failure isn't failure; it is one more way you have learned so you can be better at what you do the next time."

What you need to know

✓ The most effective leaders demonstrate a passion for their subject.

✓ People like to follow optimists.

✓ Real leaders genuinely believe they can positively impact their people, their customers, and their organization—and their self-confidence is contagious.

✓ Remember: body language and non-verbal cues send clear signals that convey a positive or negative image of the person.

*"When you confront
a problem, you begin
to solve it."*

Rudy Giuliani

CHAPTER 10

... Bring Me Solutions

"Would you rather read somebody else's book, or write your own story?"
– Unknown

"Frank, you mentioned that one of your top ten leadership traits was being solution oriented," said Duncan. "What did you mean by that?"

"Many years ago, while I was a graduate student in business school, I had an advisor who hated giving us answers; he made us figure out the problem ourselves. He called that 'training in critical thinking,' pointing out that when we had graduated and moved into the real world, we would not have a professor standing over us always ready to bail us out. Whenever a student would present a problem in one of their case studies, he would write on the blackboard: DBMP—BMS. As we quickly learned, this was short for, *Don't Bring Me Problems—Bring Me Solutions.* I cannot tell you how many times I have used that directive in the ensuing 30 years. It teaches your direct-reports to be solution—oriented, and as we've already discussed, one of the duties of a good leader is to train and empower his or her people to be results-driven.

The more you can guide your people to be self-sufficient the more they will grow in their job satisfaction and the more time you will have to concentrate on what only you as the leader should be doing."

"Does it work, this DBMP—BMS thing?" asked Duncan.

"It certainly does," I said. "I have trained my people so they now know what it means. Of course, I would never advocate using it if your employee simply doesn't know how to do his job, or to abdicate my managerial responsibility. But whether at Devlyn Optical or Rotary, if I know the person has the ability to solve the problem—maybe even in an inventive way I would never have thought of—I pull the card out of my desk drawer that says DBMP—BMS and simply hold it up in front of them."

"I bet it also reduces your stress level," said Sue.

"Yes, it does," I agreed. "And it prevents the subordinate from taking *their* problem and making it *mine*. I think I heard that once described as having the monkey put on my back; I don't need any more monkeys on my back, thank you very much."

"Perhaps it's because we were a large, engineer-driven corporate entity, but DuPro taught us to use a more scientific approach to problem solving," said Duncan.

"What do you mean 'scientific approach'?" I asked.

"There were several ways we would attack the problem," he explained. "We often used the 'divide and conquer' method, which broke down the issue into smaller more easily-solvable problems. We also employed the 'hill climbing' technique. Imagine you were climbing a very steep hill: you can't even bear looking at the summit, so you look just one step ahead and your goal is to make that step, thus moving one step closer to conquering the hill. So it is with this problem-solving method: you set mini goals that move you closer to the larger goal. At other times, we would use root cause analysis. That is where we examined how we got into this situation—the root cause—and then attempted to solve the problem by eliminating the factors that caused it in the first place."

"One of the things I learned from being club president is that some people expected me to be the expert on *everything*," Bob recalled. "At first, I fell into the trap of feeling I had to be able to answer every question and solve every problem. But I soon learned—thanks to some advice from Sue here—that we sometimes have to be creative and flexible to find solutions. And if that fails, there is nothing wrong in saying, 'I don't have a solution for that.'"

"You learned a valuable lesson, Bob." I said. "I often tell Rotary leaders that they need to work on their 'street smarts.' At first, I think they thought I was talking about acting like gang members. So I had to explain what I meant. I am saying we need to be flexible, able to respond quickly and creatively. More than once I have shown up to give what a conference organizer has told me for months would be a 20-minute speech on The Rotary Foundation, and right before I go on, they tell me the conference is running late so I only have 10 minutes—and then the speaker before me speaks about the Foundation. What I call street smarts is knowing that to be effective, I should change topics, adjust my presentation, and develop a feel for what is needed at that moment.

"They don't teach 'street smarts' in books—although in hindsight, I think my business school professor had them in mind when he taught us DBMP—BMS. Let me give you an example that David Forward told me about. Back in 1981, there was a lull in the civil war in Lebanon. So Dave organized a campaign to collect toys, clothes, and relief supplies for the thousands of children living in Lebanese orphanages because of the war. He arranged for the Rotary Club of Beirut to partner in the project and help distribute the gifts. Dave planned everything superbly—right down to obtaining a letter of introduction from the Lebanese Ambassador to Washington, which essentially said Customs should not try to collect import duty.

"What he did not know was that the airport was still under the control of the Palestinians, and when he tried to go through Customs with the enormous shipment, a PLO official demanded $5,000 in cash. When Dave confidently showed the militia supervisor his embossed letter from the ambassador, the gun-toting officer told him the PLO was still at war with the Lebanese government, and if Dave knew what was good for him, he would not be waving that document around. 'This is not Lebanon. This is PLO territory,' he said."

"Wow, that would have gotten *my* attention," said Sue. "So what happened?"

"David asked for, and received, permission to consult the person from the Beirut Rotary Club who was waiting outside," I continued. "He told him about the problem, and his greeter followed him back into Customs where he assured the official they would be back in the morning. The Lebanese Rotarian told David to just relax and sleep well; that he would find a solution to the problem the next day. Early the following morning, he picked up David from his hotel and drove him to meet a fellow Beirut Rotarian, who happened to be a senior official with the United Nations' local office. He had already begun the process of issuing new airbills, changing the consignee from the Rotary Club of Beirut to UNICEF-Beirut. 'Now it is diplomatic cargo,' he told David. 'Even the PLO would not dare intercept that.' Within an hour, David was on the way to Beirut Airport following a gray-and-white United Nations truck, which was then used for the rest of his stay as he distributed the supplies to needy children at orphanages all over the city.

"You see, that Rotarian from Beirut, and his friend with UNICEF, could easily have thrown up their hands and cried, 'Oh, this is terrible! How dare the PLO do this! How are we ever going to come up with $5,000?' But they were used to thinking fast—just to have survived the past 10 years of civil war. They had street smarts. They focused not on the problem but on finding a solution."

"That's quite a story," Bob observed. "I hadn't thought about this before, but I can see a correlation between hard skills and soft skills now. When we have a software development problem, there is usually no *one way* to solve it; we need to come at the problem from every possible angle, sometimes boring down many, many levels to try to understand why something is not working the way we intended. I am used to that approach; that's been my job since I left college. Now I can see that being a leader on many occasions calls for outside-the-box thinking which might include bringing in others to brainstorm all possible solutions. I guess leaders need to be as flexible as it takes to solve the problem, right?"

"You are right," I said. "We know there will *always* be problems for us to solve. Our job is to analyze the issue: What is the problem? When is it occurring? What are the root causes of the problem? What are the consequences if it continues? What would happen if we did nothing? If you are facing multiple problems, analyze them to determine which ones should be solved first. Next, explore possible approaches to solve the problem. It could be one of the analytical methods Duncan measured, or the 'street smarts' process I mentioned, or perhaps it calls for a brainstorming session from your entire team. Then you implement the plan that is best defined by the question *who does what?* As a leader, it is then your responsibility to monitor the progress to the ultimate determination that the problem has been solved. Finally—and this is important—is the step I'll call 'celebration time.' It is important that you bring your team together to celebrate the success of the operation by giving all of them honest, sincere recognition and appreciation for the good results. Everybody likes good news, and even if you just buy the team pizza one lunchtime, you will be sending a powerful signal to them that they can—and should—be a part of problem solving."

"I'd like to go back to your point about knowing there will always be *some* problem to deal with," said Duncan. "One of the exercises we had to run at DuPro was a simulated crisis. Every couple of years, they would send those of us in senior management on a retreat. We would be put in teams and given various assignments with a computer-generated problem. Look at how Johnson & Johnson earned such plaudits when the Tylenol crisis occurred. Do you think the day that began was when their leadership asked what they should do next? Contrast that to how British Airways suffered international humiliation because its senior management had not put a contingency plan in place when Terminal 5 opened at Heathrow Airport.

"I am not suggesting that a Rotary club president need prepare for such momentous disasters as those incidents, but part of good leadership is asking 'What if . . . ?' You know, 'What if our normal meeting place burned down?' or 'What if Frank Devlyn's flight was cancelled as he was en route to speak at our Rotary Foundation banquet?' By asking the question 'What if?' you show your team members the importance of planning and anticipating problems—and can plan solutions for those problems long before they occur."

What you need to know

✓ Remember DBMP-BMS: Don't Bring Me Problems— Bring Me Solutions!

✓ Leaders train and empower their people to be solution-oriented.

✓ Scientific problem-solving methods include:
   • Divide and Conquer
   • Hill Climbing
   • Root Cause Analysis.

✓ Leaders are not afraid of saying "I don't have a solution for that."

✓ Effective leaders have 'street smarts,' they are ready to adapt to changing times and be creative and flexible with their problem solving.

✓ Not every problem needs an immediate solution.

✓ Involve your team in brainstorming possible solutions. Sometimes you need to bore down several levels below a team member's initial suggestion.

✓ Leaders plan for serious problems by asking the question, "What if . . .?"

"If your actions inspire others to dream more, learn more, do more and become more, you are a leader."

John Quincy Adams,
6th President of the United States

CHAPTER 11

The Visionary Leader

"The future belongs to those who see possibilities before they become obvious."
– John Scully, former CEO of Apple Computer and Pepsi

"I think of those people as true visionaries," said Sue. "They are constantly looking ahead, thinking ahead, and planning ahead for the best and worst circumstances."

"They have to," I volunteered. "Because the only way an organization, regardless of whether it is a multinational corporation or a 10-member Rotary club, can progress is when its leader has a clear vision of the future and communicates it to the team.

"I believe that vision is one of the most endearing qualities of a leader. The very first thing a leader asks him- or her-self is, 'What do we believe in, where are we heading, and how are we going to get there?' It's like Duncan's analogy of flying an airplane: if you don't know where you are going, how in the world are you going to get there?"

"I can tell you from personal experience, there were a few times as a student pilot when I wasn't quite sure where I was, and I can tell you, it was not a comfortable feeling," Duncan chipped in.

"When the person at the top has an exciting vision, that is transferred to people all the way down to the bottom levels of the organization, don't you agree?" asked Sue. "I think back to my days in the airline industry when Richard Branson founded Virgin Atlantic Airways. I flew to England many times on other airlines, and they all gave pretty much the same service. But Branson had a vision for making flying fun again. He began offering lounges at their airports where you could get a haircut or play video games before the flight—all free. He put beauticians on board his aircraft so business class passengers could have a massage or a facial during those long flights. But here's my point: any CEO could have had an *idea*, but the problem is transferring it to each member of the organization. On Virgin Atlantic, Branson has done that. I was on a flight from London to Cape Town one day and the crew learned the woman next to me was on her way to her wedding. When she ordered a cappuccino later on, the flight attendant had used the shaved chocolate to make a heart shape on top of the froth. That wasn't something she learned in an operations manual; that was transference of the total-care-of-the-customer-at-all-costs vision that had been passed down from the top."

"Would you say that vision is the same as goals?" asked Bob.

"Not really," I answered. "Because goals change, whereas vision seldom changes. Go back to the example we used of setting a 25-pound weight loss as a goal. You could amend that to a 20-pound loss, or perhaps increase it to a goal of losing 30 pounds while increasing your muscles mass to X. But a *vision* would describe the bigger picture of your entire healthy lifestyle. However, having said that, I agree that vision can be the motivator to set goals."

"What do you think about putting my vision right on the front page of our weekly club bulletin?" asked Bob.

"I suppose it couldn't hurt," I replied. "But be careful: true vision is much more than a few well-chosen words on the front of a bulletin, or on a plaque in the lobby of corporate headquarters. That's not *vision*, that is public relations. Ken Blanchard—author of *The One-Minute Manager* says, 'A real vision is lived, not framed.' Sue gave us an example of somebody who was able to communicate his vision for passenger service throughout the company. What other examples have you seen that portray visionary leadership?"

There was silence for a few moments as they searched their memories. Duncan spoke first: "We were a very science-driven company at DuPro, so while I worked with a lot of people who were very good at their jobs, I can't honestly say I thought of too many of them as visionaries. I think we were mostly left-brain driven, process-oriented managers. The one person I mentioned before, University of Notre Dame President Father Hesburgh, was a visionary. He told us once that the very essence of leadership is that you have a vision. He communicated to all of us his vision for us to not only graduate with good academic qualifications, but also with the mindset of living a life that mattered. That is why you will find so many people at the top level of voluntary service projects who are Notre Dame graduates. They are still living the vision Father Hesburgh passed on to them years ago when they were in college."

"I must confess, I never had a vision for living a life that mattered until I joined Rotary," admitted Bob. "When I first met you guys, the only thing I really cared about was my car, my girlfriends, and what I would be doing next weekend. The second year I was in Rotary, we had a district governor who told a great story when she made her official visit to our club. She said Alfred Nobel had made a fortune selling arms and gunpowder. Then in 1888, a newspaper erroneously published his obituary. Not too many of us have a chance to read our own obituary, but Nobel did—and he was shocked. It began, 'The merchant of death is dead,' and went on to say 'the man who grew rich by finding ways to kill more people faster than ever before, died yesterday.' Can you imagine reading that about yourself! But that single misplaced newspaper story prompted Nobel to take stock of his life and to reorder his priorities. He realized at that moment there was a difference between success and significance, and he left the bulk of his considerable fortune to create the Nobel Prize for Adult Achievement.

"Alfred Nobel's vision continues to inspire people around the world more than a hundred years later. It doesn't much matter what he did with the first 90% of his life; the legacy he left in those final eight years lives on today. And his vision inspired our past district governor to become a major donor to The Rotary Foundation, and in turn her words inspired me to change my attitude from being a 'RINO'—a Rotarian in name only— to become a Rotarian that could work to make the world a better place. And here I am, finishing my year as club president!"

It was the longest speech any of us had ever heard Bob make, and we spontaneously applauded him for his moving story.

"I cannot think of a first-person experience with a visionary leader," said Duncan. "But I do consider that Franklin Delano Roosevelt and Winston Churchill and Dr. Martin Luther King were people I considered visionaries. In their own way, they stood up during challenging times and said to us, 'We know what we stand for, we know where we're going, and we know how we're going to get there.' And you know what? We believed them. They inspired us. They caused millions of people to enlist in the cause they spoke up for, whether it was to volunteer for the war effort or to move our nation towards equal rights for all people. They communicated their vision clearly and persuasively, and we *wanted* to be a part of their dream."

"My friend Rick tells the story of when his son Nathan was in elementary school and had trouble seeing the blackboard," I began. "It turns out he had astigmatism. So they had him fitted with corrective lenses and forever afterwards, he could see clearly. Now here is my point: the world did not change, but his ability to *see* the world did. People with vision see the world differently. In every example that you just cited: Richard Branson, Alfred Nobel, Martin Luther King, Jr.—they saw the world differently and communicated their vision to their team and the world beyond. Walt Disney—a visionary by any account—said, 'If you can dream it, you can do it' and who among us even today would not agree that it must have been amazing to have worked on his team?"

"This has been a wonderful time for me," said Sue. "I remember when I was in high school math class, my teacher told me it wasn't good enough to put down the right answer; she would write in red pen, 'Show your work.' She wanted to see how I got from here to there. It seems it is the same with leadership: it's not enough to just have the answers; I need to show my people how we are getting from here to there. We need to show our work."

"Good point," I said. "I don't want to be overly dramatic, but to succeed today, we need to demonstrate our skills as leaders. In the workplace, being the boss worked 50 years ago, but today an autocratic approach will likely lead to a revolving door of good employees—and a heart attack for yourself. In the voluntary sector, people have so many options available that if you don't give them a reason to *want* to participate, you will fail in achieving anything worthwhile. We have a worldwide fellowship of distinguished business, professional and community leaders from whom we can learn countless attributes and skills. The Rotary Revolution is 1.2 million such people in 175 countries around the world. Can you *imagine* what we can learn from 1.2 million colleagues who know that real happiness comes from fellowship and personal integrity and serving others? The skills we have talked about today are the greatest gift we can give our employees and fellow Rotarians: they are the keys to success, today and into the future."

What you need to know

✓ Leaders have a clear vision of where they, their department and their organization will be in the future—and how they are going to get there.

✓ Leaders ask: What do we believe in, where are we heading, and how are we going to get there? Then they communicate that to the entire team.

✓ Goals can change, but vision rarely does.

✓ Leaders have made a commitment to living a life that matters.

✓ Visionary leaders inspire their followers and motivate them to be a part of the dream.

✓ The world doesn't change, but how they *see* the world changes.

"It is not the strongest of the species that survive, nor the most intelligent, but the one most responsive to change."

Charles Darwin

Conclusion

L eadership is not a skill reserved for those with impressive titles or employees to manage. The preceding pages have described the skills needed for effective leadership at every level, and all that remains is for you to unlock the power that lies within you and follow the ten simple rules of SuperStar Leaders. Each of us has been endowed with the potential to lead, and as author John Ortberg suggests, "When you receive a great gift there are two ways to respond: one is to say, 'This is too valuable to use.' The other is to say, 'This is too valuable NOT to use.'"

The key to successful leadership today is not coercion, it is persuasion. To be considered a true and effective leader, one needs to earn the respect of those at all levels of the hierarchical pyramid. Having the skills and knowledge to do the job is important, but not as vital as integrity, resourcefulness, vision, mentoring, communications skills and building relationships.

In the narrative, Duncan mentioned how he believed continuing education was so important that just weeks before retiring from his 43-year career, he signed up for a skills enhancement seminar. Leaders say they can never get enough learning. Rotarians already are leaders, and they participate in "continuing education" every week. They interact with community leaders and discuss how they can make the business environment more ethical, their community vibrant, and their world more peaceful. Rotarians come from such a wide variety of countries, cultures, and professions and they understand the need for mutual understanding and respect across these barriers. Each week, they also participate in meetings with speakers who run the gamut from political leaders to corporate chieftains to noted intellectuals. The value of the knowledge Rotarians learn from their diverse weekly speakers can only be described as priceless. The weekly meetings give them the opportunity to learn more about themselves, to learn from others, and to expand their horizons.

Indeed, it was a Rotary program—RYLA, the Rotary Youth Leadership Award seminars for teenagers—that led to the Institute for Leadership. Past RI Vice President "Sonny" Brown and some of his club members noted how Rotary counselors were challenged by the young people to discover what was really important in their lives. They returned from RYLA more inspired and more involved in other Rotary programs and activities because of the benefits they recognized by training the RYLA participants. So they designed a "RYLA for Rotarians," as a membership benefit at a reasonable price that they could not find anywhere else.

The preceding pages made much of the differences between the old-style authoritarian boss and the type of leader that is effective today. Changing styles are required for the changing world in which we live—and one of the attributes of a true leader is the ability to keep up with the fast-paced developments in technology, competition, and attitudes.

Consider, for example, that the parents or grandparents of those entering the workforce today considered their job to be virtually a contract that would last until retirement. Contrast that with a recent US Department of Labor report which showed one in four American workers had been in their job for less than one year. The study revealed that the average person entering the workforce today will have 10-14 jobs by their 38th birthday. In fairness, many employers long ago abandoned the safety net that assured workers of a job for life, so it is perhaps only natural that workers who have witnessed this change now look out for Number One and see nothing wrong with switching jobs frequently.

Any employer worries about the high cost of employee turnover, so having a leader that workers respect and enjoy working with—a leader who communicates enthusiasm and self-development within his or her team—is an invaluable asset.

Managers and bosses don't really care what their followers want because their focus is on getting results *their* way. But leaders strive to learn how to communicate on the same level as their followers. Today's 21-year-old has watched 20,000 hours of television, talked 10,000 hours on a telephone, and played 10,000 hours of video games. The very first text message was sent in 1992; today, the number of daily text messages exceeds the population of the planet. That same average 21-year-old has already sent 250,000 emails and text messages—and evidence that the latter is the preferred communications channel for young people can be seen in the fact there is now a National Text Messaging Championship—complete with a $25,000 prize!

Now imagine the manager who was trained in the fine art of letter writing. Without changing his own communicating habits, he will never connect with his people.

And 'connecting with his or her people' is what leaders strive to achieve. "The essence of leadership is not the leader, but the relationship," wrote Joseph Rost of University of San Diego in his book, *Leadership in the Twenty-First Century*.[4] Rost defines leadership as "an influence relationship among leaders and followers who intend real changes that reflect their mutual purposes." In his own treatise *The New Face of Leadership*, Fort Hays State University's Curtis L. Brungardt adds, "Rost reminds us that leadership is not what leaders do. Rather, leadership is what leaders and followers do together for the collective good. In today's society, leaders operate in a shared-powered environment with followers. No longer does a single leader have all the answers and the power to make substantial changes. Instead, today we live in a world where many people participate in leadership, some as leaders and others as followers. Only when we all work together can we bring about successful changes for our mutual purposes."

It should be obvious that the objectives for leaders this book described were painted with a broad brush. For example, if the reader aspires to rise through the ranks of his or her Rotary club—and then into district roles and beyond, it is important to remember that the followers will be volunteers. Informal organizations such as Rotary convey the personal interests of their members. The leader has no real power, and thus must rely on being able to inspire and persuade his followers to pursue his agenda, otherwise the follower can either quit, or remain passive and unresponsive, leaving the leader frustrated and unaccomplished. At the other end of the spectrum is the militaristic organization, such as the army or a police department. Leaders in these groups, while still needing the traits described in this book, can employ a more

---

[4] Praeger Publisher, 1993

authoritarian style with subordinates. Somewhere in the middle of the continuum is the corporate entity. Employees are not as free to simply walk away as they are in voluntary organizations, and yet a supervisor will rarely succeed by using a dictatorial management style. The key is for the leader to be aware of the situation in which she is operating, and to then adapt her approach, as professional speakers say, to *know your audience.*

James MacGregor Burns, renowned author and authority on leadership studies, introduced a normative element: an effective Burnsian leader will unite followers in a shared vision that will improve an organization and society at large. Burns calls leadership that delivers "true" value, integrity, and trust *transformational leadership.*[5]

Can there be a more worthy goal than to be considered a transformational leader, a person with a vision for taking the status quo and making it better? Can there be a better way to raise one's own self esteem than to have clearly communicated that vision to others on your team—a team with people who like you and are passionate about achieving your goals? Can there be a more uplifting and enjoyable experience than following a transformational leader, one who signs his work with excellence and puts enthusiasm and energy into everything she does?

Five birds were sitting on a telephone wire and three of them decided to fly away. How many birds are still sitting on the wire? The answer is five: the three *decided* to fly away, but they took no action. So it is with many of us. We attend a seminar, listen to self-improvement tapes, or read a book and *decide* we need to do something different to make us better

5 *Wikipedia,* 2008

or more effective at what we do. But to truly transform ourselves we need to take action, not just "decide."

Real leaders take responsibility and are accountable for their actions, so the rest is up to you. In his book, *Sales SuperStars*, David C. Forward gave a secret to success that certainly applies to leaders. The secret is a 10-word sentence, and each word has just two letters and one syllable. Are you ready to be a SuperStar Leader? *Are you ready for the secret? If it is to be, it is up to me*!

Good luck!

Leadership Self-Evaluation

Rank yourself on the following scale:
0 = Never, 1 = Rarely, 2 = Occasionally, 3 = Mostly, 4 = Always

1	When our club or district fails to meet a goal, I tend to look for the "Why?" rather than the "Who?"	
2	When I encounter a problem, my initial thought is, "Who can I ask for help?" rather than "How do I solve this?"	
3	I sincerely want to end my year with the club/district stronger than when I started the year.	
4	I am confident that my leadership skills in Rotary will help me be more effective in my professional & personal life.	
5	I believe my club/district will be more successful if I can help develop the leadership skills of those around me.	
6	I have assembled my own mentors to give me encouragement and advice.	
7	I fully understand why I am in my leadership position and am confident I will succeed.	
8	I have identified future potential club/district leaders and have pledged to mentor them.	
9	I rely more on the power of persuasion and my personality than on my title to get others to achieve my objectives.	
10	I derive personal reward from helping others.	
11	I have written "SMART" goals for my year, broken down into monthly or weekly segments—and have communicated these to my team.	

12	When people ask me for advice, I usually turn the question back to encourage them to explore possible solutions.	
13	I am not afraid to propose ideas that our club/district has never tried before.	
14	I attend as many district, zone, and RI conferences, workshops, training- and idea meetings as possible.	
15	When someone on my team fails to deliver on an objective, I try to "take out" the problem, rather than being angry at the person.	
16	I frequently use active listening skills.	
17	I constantly look for ways to make the Rotary experience more fun and rewarding for my members.	
18	I am completely confident that my members see me as a paragon of integrity and trustworthiness.	
19	I see myself as committed to excellence in my Rotary leadership position.	
20	I do not criticize or gossip about people to others.	
21	Each member of my club, if asked outside my presence, would say I show loyalty and respect to others.	
22	The people on my leadership team share my commitment to excellence, integrity, and values.	
23	I don't always jump to give my opinion. I often defer my response until I have had time to investigate all possibilities and options.	
24	I prefer to give praise for our accomplishments while taking personal accountability for our club/district shortcomings.	
25	I never see failure as failure, but only as a lesson in how not to do something next time.	
	Total Score:	

Scoring

95 or higher: You are a leadership superstar!

89 – 94: You're a good leader.

83 – 88: Moderate leadership skills.

77 – 82: Time for further study.

76 or lower: This book was written for you!

Make *Frank Talk* work
for your club and district

Tens of thousands of Rotarians the world over have used *Frank Talk* to tell the story of Rotary—and help bring in new members.

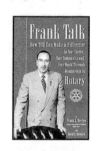

Many went on to buy *Frank Talk II* to show their members how to change with the times do their part to *energize* their club and make members more active and involved—and keep wavering members from leaving!

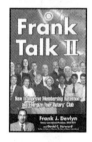

Next came *Frank Talk on Our Rotary Foundation*. This valuable resource educates Rotarians about the work of The Rotary Foundation and motivates them to be more supportive of their club and district Foundation goals.

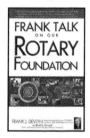

Now you can add *Frank Talk on Leadership* to your library! This valuable resource defines the differences between *managing* and *leading*. It shows readers how they can be more effective at creating support for their goals and can develop loyal, enthusiastic teams—whether at work, in Rotary, or in community groups. If you ever had a dream and wondered how you can get from *here* to *there*, this is a must-read!

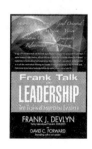

Look at how you can save money by ordering copies for each member.

	Frank Talk	Frank Talk 2	Frank Talk 3	Frank Talk 4	
Single copy	$13.95	$13.95	$13.95	$13.95	
10-24 copies	$ 8.95	$ 8.95	$ 8.95	$ 8.95	**Save 36%!**
25-99 copies	$ 5.95	$ 5.95	$ 5.95	$ 5.95	**Save 57%!**
100 + copies*	$ 4.95*	$ 4.95*	$ 4.95*	$ 4.95*	**Save 65%!**

*The four titles can be combined, in lots of 25, and still receive this rate for orders totaling 100 or more. Prices are in US$.

To order:

Use our secure sites online:
www.FrankTalkBooks.com or www.FrankDevlyn.org

OR

Call +1.856.988.1738

OR

Fax +1.856.988.0511

The Rotary Leadership Institute

The Rotary Leadership Institute (RLI) is a worldwide grass-roots organization of Rotary districts whose mission is to provide a quality education in Rotary knowledge and leadership skills for POTENTIAL leaders of Rotary CLUBS. RLI believes that successful leadership of our clubs requires BOTH good leadership skills and a comprehensive knowledge of Rotary. Excellent club leadership is essential to the future of Rotary.

Those wishing to learn more about RLI are urged to contact RLI International Chair David Linett at ginlin@aol.com or any Regional Vice-Chair around the world.

Institute for Leadership

The Institute for Leadership is a highly professional, interactive two-day event whose mission is to provide Rotarians a leadership program that will enhance their personal growth and further develop their leadership skills to better serve and benefit their communities, their families and their business endeavors. Its goal is to awaken a greater passion for leading and serving through Rotary's avenues of service so that the Rotary motto "Service Above Self" comes alive in every Rotarian.

For more information view www.instituteforleadershipinfo, contact Sonny Brown at the following numbers: 915-584-5511 phone, sonny@sonnybrown.com or ibrown@elp.rr.com